STAND TALL:
ESSAYS ON LIFE AND SERVANT LEADERSHIP

KELVIN A. REDD

Published by the Greenleaf Center for Servant Leadership
770 Pawtucket Drive, Westfield, IN 46074
www.greenleaf.org
Printed in the United States of America

Book and cover design by Joe Hunt

STAND TALL

ESSAYS ON LIFE AND SERVANT LEADERSHIP

KELVIN A. REDD

THE GREENLEAF CENTER FOR SERVANT LEADERSHIP

To my late Grandmother Essie Mae Brundidge,
a real servant leader and a Crown of Life.

Table of Contents

Forward

I read Kelvin Redd's *Stand Tall: Essays on Life and Servant Leadership* in one sitting for several reasons:

1. Kelvin is an unusual person and I value his thoughts.
2. He left a great job at Synovus, where he had a bright future with a company that was named by *Fortune* magazine to be the "Best Place to Work in America," in order to go to the Pastoral Institute to take on a challenging assignment.
3. In his own way, Kelvin is seeking meaning and purpose for his life. The Pastoral Institute appealed to his own needs to learn, grow, and serve others, and to use his God-given talents to speak and to write.

Kelvin is a great observer of people, and he is able to offer others the lessons on servant leadership that he sees around him at the Pastoral Institute. I know that you will learn much about servant leadership and about yourself as you read his essays, and I hope you will join those of us who believe that servant leadership can change our world.

William B. Turner
Author, Founding Member of
the Pastoral Institute

Introduction

My purpose in writing this book is to share some thoughts on life and servant leadership—the greatest leadership philosophy in the world. My intent is to focus on the practical aspects of life, and the ways in which servant leadership can transform the world.

Some surveys reveal that 87 percent of American workers are unhappy with their jobs. Yet Americans spend an average of 46 hours a week at work! To me, that is an awful lot of time to spend where one is not happy. It is also a waste of energy and the gifts God has bestowed upon us.

I have spent years studying what makes "the great" great. My bookshelves at home are full of leadership books and biographies of amazing men and women. But a lot of what I have learned has come from life itself. My own knowledge and experience have led me to believe that servant leadership is indeed the most effective leadership philosophy in the world.

How did I arrive at this conclusion? I was raised by servant leaders—my parents and my late grandmother. My father, James B. Redd, is an extraordinary man. He was the lone chemistry and physics teacher in the Phenix City (Alabama) School System from 1969–1989, and for 15 of those years, he was the head basketball coach at Central High School. Recently, he was inducted into the Chattahoochee Valley Sports Hall of Fame in Columbus, Georgia. Growing up I heard the best motivational speeches just sitting at his knees. My mother, Marie Redd, is caring, compassionate, strong-willed, and a great listener. She is also the most giving person I know. She is truly the backbone of our family. I wouldn't expect anything less because the person she is today is due to one woman, her mother and my late grandmother, Essie Mae Brundidge. My grandmother was amazing. She was a servant leader long before the term was ever coined. I've always felt that there should be a picture of her in the dictionary under the definition of grandmother.

I have also worked with servant leaders. For 13 years I worked for Synovus, in Columbus, Georgia, a company *Fortune* magazine rated in 1999 as "The Best Place to Work in America." In a sense, one could say that I have been on a national championship team. Words of wisdom from meetings led by Jimmy Blanchard and Bill Turner are still with me today. One of my favorite leaders during those years was my first manager, H. Lynn Drury.

Because I was raised by servant leaders, and have worked with servant leaders, it is no surprise that I have always valued servant leadership. As the Director of the Center for Servant Leadership at the Pastoral Institute in Columbus, Georgia, I get to live my passion for the topic by sharing it every day with others.

You may be asking yourself, "What is servant leadership and where did the term servant leadership come from?" The term "servant leadership" was coined by the noted management philosopher Robert K. Greenleaf in his original essay, *The Servant as Leader,* which was first published in 1970. Greenleaf's definition of servant leadership was:

> The servant-leader *is* servant first… It begins with the natural feeling that one wants to serve, to serve *first*. Then conscious choice brings one to aspire to lead. That person is sharply different from one who is *leader* first, perhaps because of the need to assuage an unusual power drive or to acquire material possessions…The leader-first and the servant-first are two extreme types. Between them there are shadings and blends that are part of the infinite variety of human nature.
>
> The difference manifests itself in the care taken by the servant-first to make sure that other people's highest priority needs are being served. The best test, and difficult to administer, is: Do those served grow as persons? Do they, *while being served*, become healthier, wiser, freer, more autonomous, more likely themselves to become servants? And, what is the effect on the least privileged in society? Will they benefit or at least not be further deprived?

When I was hired as the Associate Director of the Center for Servant Leadership at the Pastoral Institute, the first thing I did was try to learn all I could about my new division. One of the first pieces of information I came across was Bill Turner's *10 Characteristics of a Servant Leader.* I immediately wanted to conduct a workshop on the 10 characteristics, but I first needed his permission. I called his office and asked if I could meet with him. He graciously said yes and to come on down.

During our meeting, I told Mr. Turner of my desire to conduct a workshop on his *10 Characteristics.* He said that he did not mind at all. However, thinking back on it, he said, "If I had it to do all over again, I expect these characteristics would be different." He went on to say that he supposed everyone has his own characteristics of a servant leader.

The conversation that day in Mr. Turner's office really made me think. Did I have my own list of the characteristics of a servant leader? If so, what were they? Later, I posed this question to a couple of my co-workers and after much discussion we decided to develop the Center for Servant Leadership's characteristics of a servant leader, although we decided to refer to them as qualities.

We scheduled a two-hour meeting for the following Friday morning. Personally, I thought it would be a no-brainer. I had my 10 qualities and figured my co-workers would be in agreement with them. Not so fast, my friend. It did not happen that way. In fact, it took us several months to come up with not only our 10 qualities, but also the Pastoral Institute's definition of servant leadership.

The following are the Center for Servant Leadership's *Qualities of a Servant Leader* headed by the Center's definition of servant leadership:

> Servant leadership is a lifelong journey that includes the discovery of one's self, the desire to serve others and a commitment to lead.

1. *Trustworthy.* Ethical and honest.

Do you behave with integrity? Are you ethical? Can the people in your sphere of influence trust you? Have you ever worked with someone or for someone you didn't trust? What happens when that person suddenly starts being nice to you? It's a little unsettling, isn't it? Trust is the cornerstone in all relationships.

2. *Self-Aware.* Open to receiving feedback.

How well do you know yourself? What are your strengths? What are your weaknesses? Are you using your strengths for the good of society? Are you in the right career field? Are you open to receiving honest feedback about yourself? When assessing who you are, can you accept the brutal facts of reality? As Bill Turner so often says, "A person cannot be an effective leader if he doesn't know who he is."

3. *Humble.* Overcoming our own self-centeredness; when things are for and about others and not for and about me. Repeat this to yourself: "It's not about me."

4. *Caring.* Meeting the needs of others; showing compassion and unconditional love.

Averaging 46 hours a week on the clock, most Americans spend more time at work than they do with their spouse or children. How well do you know the people you see every day? Do you display random acts of kindness or consistent acts of kindness? Remember, until people know you care about them, they don't care how much you know.

5. *Visionary.* Courageous leadership, inspiring, imaginative.

What is your vision? What is your organization's, department's or family's vision? Have you shared the vision with the people in your sphere of influence? Do you want to lead people to the next level? If so, what does the next level look like? As it says in Proverbs 29:18, "Where there is no vision, the people perish."

6. *Empowering Others.* To be committed to growing and helping others grow.

As a leader, you cannot do it all by yourself. It is the responsibility of the leader to make sure that everyone on the team knows his role, learns his role and is allowed to perform his role (without unnecessary oversight or interference). This lets people know that you respect them and that they are accountable for their actions. I once heard a speaker say, "One of man's biggest fears is when he is not in control." No one wants to be micromanaged.

7. *Relational.* To listen and be inclusive, empathic and persuasive.

"It's all about relationships," says Dr. Ron King, Executive Director and CEO of the Pastoral Institute. Servant leaders have an understanding heart. They listen and respect the differences in others. Servant leaders strive to get in touch with the inner you. Servant leaders like you for you, not because of your parking spot, your corner office, the title you hold or the badge you wear.

8. *Competent.* To know the issues and have the skills needed for the job.

As Kouzes and Posner state in *The Leadership Challenge*, "Leadership competence refers to the leader's track record and the ability to get things done." If the leader can perform, he will have followers. Richard may be the nicest guy in the world, but if he cannot perform the tasks and responsibilities placed before him, he will not succeed and neither will the department, the team, or the organization which he has been asked to lead.

9. *Good Steward.* To be responsible for resources entrusted to you.

Being a good steward means doing your best for the organization, taking care of the environment, and developing and using your God-given gifts in order to make the world a better place. It is a privilege to have the opportunities bestowed upon us and we should take care of our resources, whatever they may be.

10. *Community Builder.* To create a sense of value and connectedness.

Building others up and not tearing them down; bringing them together in order to make them feel like a part of the process.

Actually becoming a servant leader is a goal you may never reach. This is simply because becoming a servant leader is, indeed, a striving, a journey or a process. But what a wonderful journey it is! Somewhere on this journey you will begin to have a keen sense of self, and it is only when one understands self that one can truly begin to understand others. From this comes the commitment to lead. I call it a "want to" or the desire to serve others because it is at this point that one realizes it is not about "me."

I hope this book of essays will help you to think about your own journey as a servant leader, and how you can make a difference by helping others.

A Mother's Love

Abraham Lincoln once said, "All that I am or ever hope to be, I owe to my angel Mother." That's how I feel.

I'd like to introduce you to an amazing woman, my mother, Marie Redd. She's someone with whom I am incredibly close. Once, when a friend of mine told me that I was a Momma's boy, I disputed him, but after much thought, I realized he was right. I am very much a Momma's boy and proud of it.

I call my mother every day, beginning each morning on my drive to work. I have to make sure she's okay. If she is okay, then I know that everything else is just fine. I do this because Mom is the backbone of our family.

I've always been able to count on her. That's why I don't want to let her down. She was never the strictest disciplinarian but she always had a way of leading me to do the right thing.

Mom was the first person to encourage me to do public speaking. She told me early and often that I had a gift, and that I should use it. There was a time in my life when I was reluctant to speak. But it was Mom who always discouraged me from giving up. She'd always say, "Son, if you don't use it, you will lose it."

Mom has incredible faith, something she no doubt learned from her mother. For instance, several years ago, a lump was discovered in Mom's breast. Needless to say, I became quite worried. I asked her how she felt and if she was worried. She told me that she felt fine and she wasn't worried at all. This was the first time I really noticed her faith. I was amazed. In the end, everything did turn out to be okay.

When the doctor discovered that my sister had a hearing problem and would have to wear two hearing aids, Mom immediately took charge. She worked diligently with her every night after school to make sure her homework was completed. Mom was in constant contact with her teachers. She didn't want my sister missing out on things that she may not have heard the teacher say during class.

One of my mother's ambitions in life was to attend college. Mom gave up that ambition to raise a family and to work. I hope she can take some comfort in the fact that although she never graduated from college, she did raise two kids who earned bachelor and master's degrees and one of whom is steadily approaching a doctoral degree.

My mother has taught me so much. When I become cantankerous, Mom tells me that's not the way to be. When I do well at something, she applauds me. I know that Mom loves me unconditionally. She's a true servant leader. She's loving, kindhearted, and giving. She has taught me never to give up and to follow my dreams. For that, I am most thankful. I love you, Mom!

Remember Who You Are

During my workshop *Servant Leadership: The World's Greatest Leadership Philosophy*, I often ask participants to identify a leader in their life—that one person who always told them they were special and made them feel really good about themselves. I want them to recall the one person who told them they could "climb the highest mountain," if they put their mind to it. That one who they could always count on when times got tough. It was because of this leader's inspiration that they became the person they are today. Can you, too, think of that person in your life? Who did you count on when times got tough?

Many of us have been blessed to have had a person in our lives who has played a significant role in developing us into who we are right now. Perhaps that person is a mother, father, grandmother, grandfather, coach or teacher. They taught us many of life's most important lessons: how to handle difficult people and situations, how to rise above mistakes, and in many cases, how to deal with tragedies. In my case, when I'm facing a tough time, I can hear my father telling me to "Stand tall."

One of my favorite animated movies is *The Lion King*. It's filled with lots of lessons, but there is one I would like to share with anyone who may be facing a challenging time.

The Lion King is about a young lion cub named Simba who grew up idolizing his father, Mufasa, the king of the Pride Lands. Mufasa began teaching Simba the ways of the world at a young age, and as is the case with many of us at certain points in our lives, all was not good in the Pride Lands. That source of "no good" and wickedness was Scar, Mufasa's brother.

Scar was lazy, good-for-nothing and jealous of his brother Mufasa. He was always trying to undermine his brother's authority. Eventually, Scar's jealousy grew so great that he killed his brother Mufasa and convinced Simba that he was to blame for his father's death. Frightened and ashamed, Simba fled the Pride Lands; however, fleeing did not stop Simba's pain in losing the seminal figure of his youth. He wandered aimlessly through the vast jungle and was very depressed and afraid. Simba was all alone now and didn't know what to do or which way to turn. Then, one day Simba looked up toward the heavens and there appeared a cloud in the form of his father Mufasa. Mufasa looked down upon his son and said, "Simba, remember who you are." At that moment Simba realized he had allowed others and his circumstances to dictate who he was instead of embracing his true identity—the king of the Pride Lands.

Are you presently facing a challenging time in your life? If so, remember who *you* are. Remember those words of wisdom shared by that leader in your life. Remember to "stand tall," and "face life head on." Will it be easy? Probably not, but that should not deter you from moving forward. You may stop in your tracks for a bit and even cry a little, but never give up. Press on toward the prize, whatever that may be, and always *remember who you are.*

Character First

Merriam-Webster's Online Dictionary defines character as "one of the attributes or features that make up and distinguish an individual." Characterfirst.com defines character as "the stable and distinctive qualities built into an individual's life which determine his or her response regardless of circumstances." A true measure of character is what you do when no one else is watching.

If character is indeed what you do when no one else is watching, then you have to admire J.P. Hayes. Hayes is a 43-year-old journeyman golfer from Appleton, Wisconsin. In 1998 Hayes won the Buick Classic and in 2002 he won the John Deere Classic.

In November 2008, while playing in a PGA qualifying golf tournament in Texas, he realized he had made a mistake. For two strokes, he had used a non-regulation golf ball—one that was not approved for competition. Hayes turned himself in and was subsequently disqualified by PGA officials. When asked by reporters why he admitted his error, Hayes simply said, "I violated a rule, and I had to take my medicine." He did not blame anyone but himself. He could have easily implicated his caddy, who actually handed him the golf balls to play on that fateful hole, but he refused to do so. Many people questioned whether it was prudent for Hayes to come forward. After all, there were no television cameras around when he played the hole. His golf shots were not witnessed by anyone else, and it was highly unlikely that anyone would know that the golf balls did not meet regulations. To make matters worse, Hayes missed out on his primary professional goal: to earn a spot on the PGA tour. Maintaining his integrity meant he had to sacrifice something important to him.

I am sure Hayes' decision will be a topic of discussion in leadership workshops for years to come. Especially since we now live in a world where poor character or even the appearance of such behavior seems to be the norm, whether it is Major League Baseball's steroid investigations or the unscrupulous activities of Wall Street tycoons like Bernard Madoff.

In conclusion, please do not think that I am being holier than thou. On the contrary, God only knows the mistakes I have made in my life. I am, however, talking about the importance of consistent acts of good behavior because it is good character that is central to an individual's success in life. Our character is the big screen on which others see us, and it is the gateway to our soul. Good character means doing the right thing because it is the right thing to do. If doing the right thing comes with a cost, do the right thing anyway.

It's All About Relationships

"We don't lead our lives in solitary confinement. We lead our lives in the open. We lead our lives in the company of others..."
– Kouzes and Posner, *A Leader's Legacy*

I love sports, and college football is my favorite. I admire the way good coaches communicate with their players. In fact, in a recent *Atlanta Journal Constitution* article, it was reported that Coach Mark Richt of the University of Georgia gave up his offensive coordinator duties to one of his assistant coaches because he wanted "to spend more time bonding with his players...and oversee the entire team during games."

According to Jim Kouzes and Barry Posner, authors of the book *A Leader's Legacy* and the bestselling book *The Leadership Challenge,* the word *follower* implies "a lack of initiative or drive or ability," while *constituent* means "someone who is an essential participant in something." If you are in a position of leadership, it is imperative that you understand your constituents need you.

The word *constituent* can have a broad connotation. For instance, you could be a supervisor for five employees; you might have four clients; or you might have three kids. Guess what—they are your constituents. What if you are a school principal? Your constituents would include the students, the faculty and the staff. (But don't forget about the parents; they depend on you, too.)

What about the business and community leaders in your immediate area? Don't you want them to support your organization? If so, how well do you know these people, and how often do you communicate with them?

As a leader, it is vital that you communicate with your constituents as much and as often as possible. "Leadership is a relationship...it requires a resonant connection with others over matters of the heart," say Kouzes and Posner in the book *A Leader's Legacy.* As Dr. Ron King, the CEO/Executive Director of the Pastoral Institute, likes to point out, "It's all about relationships."

Leadership is the skill of influence. So, how can you have influence without a personal connection? I am not talking about surface-level; on the contrary, I am talking about a deeply holistic (mind, body and soul) type of relationship whereby the leader shares who he is and seeks to know those in his sphere of influence at a deeper level. This is the type of relationship that makes it enjoyable to come to work each and every day, and it is one of the few ways to effect real change in an organization. Don't you think 40+ hours a week is an awful lot of time to spend in a place where you're not actively engaged in the lives and well-being of others?

"Hold on, Kelvin," you say. 'I don't want that type of relationship with the people I work with." Oh, no? Haven't you ever heard of the Scripture that says, "For unto whomever much is given, of him shall much be required..." (Luke 12:48, King James Version)? Besides, didn't you sign up to be a leader? Didn't you bust your hump all those years in school and climb the corporate ladder to be where you are now? Didn't you sign up to be the teacher, the vice president, the director, the principal, the coach, the superintendent, the doctor, the supervisor or team leader? I've got news for you. That project you've been so busy working on is nowhere near as important as the people you've been called upon to lead!

Perhaps you're not the "social" type. In fact, you might be an introvert like me. I know this leadership stuff is not easy. That's why leadership is a skill and it takes practice—lots and lots of practice. So, here's a solution. For starters, buy yourself a planner. Schedule time to meet and greet people, and make those important and often overlooked phone calls to your constituents. Hey, don't forget, we now live in the "hi-tech" Information Age. Instead of sending a handwritten note (which is good), a short email just to say hello can do wonders. After a while, with repetition (at least 21 straight days if you really want to make this a habit), you will have another skill. But don't stop there!

Leadership is a people business, and it is all about relationships.

Today's leaders need to be seen *and* heard. The days of sitting in the ivory tower are over. People will only follow a person they know. Do your constituents, not just the ones you like, in your sphere of influence *know* you?

Servant Leadership Is Not "Soft"

A couple of years ago, I had a meeting with a business associate. He told me that his organization was having labor-management issues, and things had gotten pretty bad between the two sides. I asked him whether his organization had ever considered implementing a servant leadership program. He looked at me incredulously and said, "No, I don't think servant leadership will work in our organization. We have too many men, and they're not used to that 'soft' stuff."

I can't say that I was surprised by his comment. I hear the "soft stuff" comment a lot. Many managers and supervisors like to refer to the financial skills side of the business as "hard" skills, and leadership, management, and supervisory skills as the "soft" skills side of the business. As you would expect, I don't agree one bit with their assessment. To me, they couldn't be farther from the truth.

That my colleague's organization was an all-male environment piqued my curiosity even more. This friend was making the assumption that servant leadership could not be implemented in a male-dominated environment. I thought his line of thinking was preposterous. I can think of men in the sports world who are in male-dominated environments but are servant leaders, and they are quite successful, too.

For instance, I believe Duke University's men's head basketball coach, Mike Krzyzewski, is a servant leader. Do you think he's soft? I do not. What about Tony Dungy, former head football coach of the NFL's Indianapolis Colts? Is he soft? I seriously doubt it. And you can't tell me that John Wooden, former head basketball coach of the UCLA Bruins, is soft. I submit to you that all of these men are servant leaders, and they have done their best and succeeded in their chosen endeavors.

Stephen Covey, author of the book *The 7 Habits of Highly Effective People*, says he once worked for a tough micromanager and didn't like that experience very much. However, when the micromanager was replaced by a servant leader, Covey says, "The servant leader who replaced him was actually tougher. That experience taught me that servant leadership is not soft or touchy-feely. It's a much tougher style because, when you set up performance agreements and become a source of help, people have to be tough on themselves. They can't just sit around and blame others."

If servant leadership is "soft" leadership, then why were two of the greatest servant leaders of the 20th century, Mahatma Gandhi and the Reverend Dr. Martin Luther King, Jr., killed? They had the desire to "stick their necks out" and do what was right in the face of institutions much bigger and stronger than they were. Few of us would dare do that.

Servant leaders can encounter a great deal of resistance because they are constantly trying to do the right thing. Since the dawn of time, those who have tried the hardest to do the right thing, have been victimized. They go against the grain, and are usually not celebrated until long after they are gone. A recent Google search netted 535,000 hits on the saying, "good guys finish last."

I strongly believe that servant leadership can be effective in any type of environment or career. Servant leadership will work whether you are a school principal, athletic director, city council person, attorney, minister, teacher or (fill in your career). All careers require use of the servant leadership philosophy, from putting others first, to using sound organizational structures, to making tough decisions, dealing with reality, providing the vision, and leading with authority. None of this is "soft."

The Boss Pleaser
Model of Leadership

The traditional top down or autocratic style is the most typical form of leadership in today's organizations. The decision making is concentrated in the hands of one individual. This one individual is called the boss (among other things). He is the one who is in control as he covets as much power as possible. Instead of serving the company, he believes his employees exist to serve him. The Center for Servant Leadership at the Pastoral Institute calls this model of leadership The Boss Pleaser Model.

The Boss Pleaser Model organizational chart looks like a pyramid. The employees are located at the bottom of the organization followed by the supervisors. Mid-level managers are situated in the middle of the chain of command. They are usually the hardest working people in the organization and typically they are also the most stressed. They feel squeezed because they are in the middle. Senior managers are located at the second highest level of the hierarchy. Many senior managers are upwardly mobile and spend the bulk of their time jockeying for position to succeed the highest ranking member of the organization. And the highest ranking person on the Boss Pleaser Model is the "Big Guy" or the CEO.

In The Boss Pleaser Model of Leadership the employees are often uptight, afraid, and indignant. They feel that their only avenue to succeed in the organization is to please the person on the next level of the pecking order. The person on the next level is typically their boss or someone who might be their future boss. Thus, they are known to "kiss up" to the person who is directly above them in rank. The old "smooch" tactic becomes a daily part of their job description.

Jack Rivers was 22 years old, intelligent, supremely confident in his abilities, very well read, and extremely outgoing. He married his college sweetheart, moved to her hometown and was in the first full month of his new job as a management trainee for XYZ Corp.

Jack learned everything he could about the company and became keenly aware of the inner workings of the organization and its key people. If only he could "get in" good with one of XYZ's eight division managers, he thought, his life would be set. As luck would have it, he would get his chance when he was chosen to shadow Keith, the Product Services Division Manager, for a day.

Jack wanted desperately to make a good impression and in the days before reporting to Keith's office, Jack made considerable efforts to learn as much as he could about the division manager. He found out where Keith lived, which church he belonged to, his favorite charities, and his hobbies.

In fact, the morning he was supposed to begin shadowing Keith, Jack had breakfast with Anthony, one of his management trainee co-workers.

"Guess where I am getting my haircut on Saturday morning?" said Jack.

"Where?" Anthony asked.

"At the barber shop on the corner of Fifth and Main," remarked Jack with a sheepish grin.

"What's so big about that?" asked a befuddled Anthony.

"That's where Keith gets his hair cut," said Jack as the corners of his mouth grew wider.

During the day with Keith, Jack was extremely attentive. He listened and asked all the right questions and did whatever he was told. He also learned a lot more about Keith than he ever thought possible—things that he thought would prove beneficial to his career advancement in the days and weeks ahead.

Employees were allowed to "dress down" or wear their business casual attire to work on Fridays, which was appreciated in the southern part of the country where XYZ was headquartered. The summers could be stifling and wearing formal attire in July was no fun.

The young male management trainees, most of whom were fresh out of college, wore polo shirts, khaki pants, and loafers on the dress-down day. They liked the casual feel and felt that they still looked "cool."

The senior managers, on the other hand, had their own uniform that they wore on Fridays. They, too, wore khaki pants, but they also wore a gosh-awful-looking plaid shirt and suede shoes to match. On the surface, this did not seem like such a big deal. After all, they were the seasoned veterans of the company and these were clothes they had always worn on casual Friday.

But on the Friday after he shadowed Keith, Jack showed up at work wearing khaki pants, a gosh-awful-looking plaid shirt and the suede shoes to match. Some of Jack's co-workers snickered behind his back. Anthony remarked that Jack looked like little Keith.

Perhaps every organization has a Boss Pleaser. He will do just about anything to gain the acceptance, recognition, and even friendship of his boss. However, at what point does one work so hard to please the boss that he loses his sense of self? There is also another factor that is deeply disturbing in the Boss Pleaser Model, and that is the power distance that is created between those at the top or near the top versus those in the middle and at the bottom of the pyramid. Where organizations should be of one heartbeat, the Boss Pleaser Model creates an us-versus-them mentality within the organization among its most valuable asset: its people. How much of a power distance have our organizations created between the CEO and their senior managers and the rest of the personnel? How many hoops must the average American worker jump through in order to feel truly comfortable and authentic while in the presence of those at the top of the pyramid?

The Fiefdom Builder: A Major Hindrance to Servant Leadership

This may surprise you. Servant leadership is not an accepted philosophy of leadership in many organizations, and there are numerous reasons why. Previously, I told you what servant leadership is. Now we will discuss what servant leadership is not and the organizational hindrances to this ancient philosophy. Servant leadership is not bringing employees coffee and donuts for breakfast or designating Fridays as casual days and allowing employees to wear blue jeans. On the contrary, it is much more and much deeper than that. Servant leadership is about having a genuine desire to meet the legitimate needs of your employees.

Robert Greenleaf, the father of servant leadership, says "…the best test, and difficult to administer, is: do those served grow as persons; do they, while being served, become healthier, wiser, freer, more autonomous, more likely themselves to become servants?" I have a question for you: in your current job, are those you lead growing as employees? Are they growing as persons? Do they have the autonomy to make decisions and do not feel micromanaged if they do? If not, why? I cannot answer these questions for you, only you can.

There's an old saying, "Everything begins and ends with leadership," so when I read statistics that indicate 43 percent of American workers leave their job because of what they perceive to be a bad boss (I loathe the word boss), that tells me that something just isn't right in the workplace. In small organizations, the problem is often at the top, but in larger organizations, the problem is often somewhere near the top. Jim Collins, the author of the book *Good To Great*, says that one of the most difficult aspects of being a leader is to look in the mirror and face reality. And in reality, there are many people in positions of leadership who exhibit less than admirable behaviors, inside and outside of the office. One very prevalent and appalling behavior in workplaces today and a major hindrance to the spread of servant leadership is what I call the "fiefdom builder."

Fiefdom builders are usually people in leadership near the top of the heap. They have surrounded themselves with "yes" men (and women). They lead by intimidation, and they hire people for the sole purpose of advancing their own careers. The office secretary becomes their watchdog. Diversity of thought is not encouraged around this type of leader. Some may think fiefdom builders are not intelligent, but that's not the case. Often polished but secretly feeling inferior, fiefdom builders are technically efficient. However, their main problem is they lack character, pure and simple. Everything is "me, me, me." They cause divisions within the team. Their only concern is what happens in their department. As long as their department looks good in the annual report, they are happy. Many of today's fiefdom builders have been "grandfathered" into their current positions. They are seldom held accountable for their negative actions. Highly street smart, they have weathered every storm that has come their way. Fiefdom builders often talk of retirement but in reality they have no plans to go anywhere. Why would they? Their job is the only place where they find an exaggerated sense of self-importance.

So, in the words of Robert Greenleaf, in your organization, are your people growing as employees? Are they growing as persons? Are they becoming healthier, wiser, freer, and more autonomous? Are their needs being met?

A House Divided

A house divided cannot stand. In order for your organization (family, workplace, city, church) to reach the heights set forth by the organization's vision, everyone must be able to work together. This does not mean you have to like everyone in the organization, but it does mean that you must treat people with respect and unconditional love. Ultimately, it is the leader who must be held responsible for creating this type of environment.

However, it is not uncommon for constituents (employees, students, parishioners, players) to have to deal with a "wannabe" leader, someone who feels as though he should have been selected as the leader. He doesn't like the idea that someone else was chosen. An organization cannot survive with this type of two-headed monster effect. In short, no one can serve two masters.

In most cases, everyone is a leader to some degree but a team must ultimately have that "one" person who is held accountable for moving the group in its desired direction. Silos—or cliques—must be avoided at all costs because they only further and enhance constituent discord. Employees begin talking about one another behind each other's backs. Players on the defensive side of the ball don't want to have anything to do with the players on the offensive side of the ball. Mom tells the child to do one thing while Dad tells the child to do another. The older members of the church resent the pastor because he favors the ideas of the younger members. Internal departmental divisions begin fighting over customers.

The movie *Remember the Titans* takes place at the recently segregated T.C. Williams High School in Alexandria, Virginia, in 1971. African-American Herman Boone is hired to replace the Caucasian head football coach. As you might imagine, or have experienced, tensions were extremely high during this time in our country's history, and the town of Alexandria and T.C. Williams High School were no different. I could easily focus on the issue of race here, but for this essay, I choose not to. The focus: the importance of having strong leadership in order to overcome organizational divisions and constituent discord.

The movie begins with T.C. Williams High School at a crossroads in 1971. The townspeople were torn on the issue of who should be the high school's head football coach. Half the town wanted Coach Boone, with the other half wanting Coach Yost. The "powers" in Alexandria held secret meetings in order to help Coach Yost regain his title of head coach. They even created unjust criteria for whether Coach Boone could keep his job by saying that if he lost one game in his first year he would be fired.

The players on the team were equally torn. They, too, were at odds on who should be their coach. From day one, the team was divided. Certain players didn't want to room with certain others at camp. Members of one group would not speak to members of the other group. One player on the offensive line wouldn't even block for his own running back. All of this, of course, led to numerous fights.

I credit both coaches for having the strength of character to build a winning team under such extreme conditions. Coach Boone and Coach Yost could have easily undermined one another and divided the team, the school, and the whole town. Coach Yost could have told some of the players to quit the team in order to make Coach Boone look bad, but he didn't do that. To his credit, Coach Yost yielded to the authority of Coach Boone. Coach Yost did not have to accept the job of defensive coordinator that Coach Boone offered him. He could have fought for the position of head coach and even if he didn't get his old title back, that pursuit alone could have set the program back decades.

I also credit Coach Boone for being a tough-minded leader who didn't fold under the pressures he was facing. Coach Boone says early in the film, "I come to win." For some, this might sound egotistical or selfish. I don't see it that way. In order to have a winning team, the leader's primary focus must be for the good of the entire team. It is detrimental to favor an average player over a good one, letting public opinion override merit. As Coach Boone said, "The best player will play…color doesn't matter." He understood the value of communication in building relationships. He knew the players did not know one another and did not care to, so from the outset as the team headed to camp, he made the players of different races sit together on the bus and made sure from that point on they would get to know each other.

In conclusion, discord often begins at the top of a hierarchy. Backbiting, gossiping, pitting one employee or one player against another, or one parishioner against another, is destructive. Playing favorites and not leading in the best interests of the team is harmful to everyone involved. Even when things appear to be going well, underlying tension often exists. If this negative attitude is pervasive in an organization, constant effort must be made to end it. If it doesn't end, "a house divided cannot stand."

This Just Ain't Right

Let's take a look at the following story. I hope it illustrates why the philosophy of servant leadership is so vitally important in the workplace.

Mary had been married to her husband, David, for seven years. They had two children, Frances, four, and seven-month-old Elizabeth. David worked as a manager for a local construction company and had been there for eight years while Mary had spent the last three years as a business analyst for a local brokerage firm. The couple routinely worked an average of 45 hours a week but never neglected loving and caring for their children. Frances attended a local preschool, and Elizabeth spent each day with her grandparents. One evening, Elizabeth began crying uncontrollably. Mary noticed that she was constantly tugging at her left ear. The next morning she took Elizabeth to see the family pediatrician. During that visit, Mary learned that Elizabeth needed surgery to remedy the aching pain and fluid build-up in both ears. The surgery was scheduled two weeks from that day.

When Mary returned to work, she immediately went to her manager's office to discuss the family issue. Mary explained that her baby was scheduled for surgery in two weeks. Although the surgery was outpatient, she wanted to know if she could have one, maybe two days, off to be with her child. Mary was not prepared for what she heard next. The answer was no, that Mary could not have one day off, let alone two. Mary told her boss that she had more than enough vacation days, if that was a concern but was told that was not the problem. Mary asked if she could swap a day with one of her co-workers, but her superior didn't budge. Her answer was the same. Mary then asked why not, and she was told the department could not afford to have anyone else out of the office during that week because they were understaffed as it was. Mary was told she was expected to be at work on the day of the surgery and on time. Mary was stunned!

Two weeks later, the family arrived at the hospital at 6:55 a.m. Around 7:40 a.m., as Mary was holding Elizabeth, one of the nurses came to get the baby to prepare her for the surgery. Understandably, the baby began to cry. She did not want to leave her mommy. The nurse asked Mary to come with her to the holding area to be with Elizabeth until they were ready to take her to the operating room. At that moment, Mary glanced at the clock on the wall. Her heart sank! It was 7:45 a.m., and she needed to leave immediately or she would be late for work. As her husband, parents, and in-laws looked on, Mary kissed her crying baby good-bye and with tears flowing down her own cheeks, she left for work.

On occasion, I have presented this story as a case study in my workshop *Servant Leadership: The World's Greatest Leadership Philosophy*. It is not uncommon for me to hear female participants say they would have stayed with their baby for the surgery and even quit the job if they had to. Mary truly regretted leaving her baby that morning, but her back was against the wall. She really needed this job. Although she and her husband both worked full-time, their household income was not sufficient for either one of them to stop working. Mary also knew she would lose her company's health insurance, which would be used to help pay for her daughter's surgery.

In his book *Carolina Way*, Dean Smith states, "Good leaders create a work environment that is like a family, where people care for one another, help one another, celebrate the success of their fellow workers. They convey this message to their employees: 'You're on my team for the rest of your life. I'm going to try to help you at every step of your career, and I'll continue to do that even if you leave the company to work elsewhere.'"

I certainly hope this will one day be the predominant thought process in our society.

Caring

One of the fundamental tenets of servant leadership is servant leaders care about their employees. Whether in the workplace or at home, all of us need this caring. Former National Championship college football coach Lou Holtz says, "One question asked by every child of every parent, every employee of every supervisor, and every student of every teacher is, 'Do you care about me?'"

Daniel had been with his company for two decades. He enjoyed his career in sales. He moved through the ranks and was promoted to his current position of Vice President.

Daniel's primary task was to get to know his employees. He wanted to familiarize himself with their strengths and weaknesses, their likes and dislikes, and what motivated them. Daniel held one-on-one meetings with his employees monthly, quarterly and annually.

The 14-member sales staff had been together for nearly eight years. Since he began managing the department, only three employees had left. One of them, Jim, left because he wasn't cut out to be a salesperson. With Daniel's help, Jim was able to begin a new career in accounting and is now the manager of the company's accounting staff of five employees.

The sales staff considered Daniel a leader, mentor and friend. He embodied characteristics of a servant leader. He was a visionary–fair, honest, trustworthy, decisive and compassionate. If one of them had a personal problem or a difficult decision he had to make, he felt comfortable going to Daniel for help and reassurance.

Because all of the employees loved working for him, there was a tendency by some in the company to think that Daniel's leadership style was "soft." This was not the case. He was a tough disciplinarian. He led by positive reinforcement and constructive, yet compassionate, criticism.

Daniel was also an avid weather-watcher. He knew each day's

forecast. On days when he knew it was going to rain or snow, he made it a point to have food catered in for lunch so his employees would not have to leave the office if they did not want to.

Daniel was a humble man. He made sure his employees were recognized for their accomplishments. During his second year as manager, his team broke all of the company's previous sales records. Top management wanted to reward him with a bonus, but Daniel saw to it that his employees received their share first.

As a leader and as a person, Daniel truly cared for his employees. He established close relationships with each of them. He felt that to do otherwise would have been insincere on his part. By exuding honesty, trust and abiding integrity, Daniel created an environment that fostered those same characteristics. His employees cared for him, too.

What about you? Do you care about the people you've been entrusted to lead? Do you care about your employees? What about your family? More importantly, do they know you care for them? Caring is essential to leadership. It is another servant leadership characteristic that must be genuine in order to be effective.

Her Biggest Fan

There were only four of us in our family; my father, mother, sister and me. We were very close and did almost everything together. My grandmothers also played a major role in our lives. They were exceedingly giving—in love and of money. We wanted for nothing. I was the first born in my family, and four and a half years later, my only sister, Krystal, was born. For some time, I was the only grandson on my father's side, which put me in an especially cherished position in the family.

I knew my sister looked up to me. How did I know? Well, let's just call it a brother's intuition. I realized I wasn't an easy brother to follow. I excelled in academics, was elected class president repeatedly, sat first chair (principal player) in band and was voted "Most Likely to Succeed" by my classmates.

I'm so proud of Krystal because not only has she endured, she has overcome. I was her hero, but now the shoe is on the other foot and she is my hero. I want you to meet her. This is her story.

Our family valued education very highly, which was to be expected since both my mother and father were valedictorians of their respective high school classes. So, it was a little disturbing when my sister's report cards weren't what my parents thought they should be.

Krystal's early years in school were a struggle. Her grades were not very good, but it wasn't due to a lack of effort. On the contrary, she worked extremely hard. That was a Redd trait passed on by our grandmother Izora. One of Krystal's elementary school teachers told my parents that Krystal should be placed in a special education class. My father, an educator, thought this was preposterous. As a result, my parents, particularly my mother, worked even harder with Krystal on her homework.

Krystal was overweight and endured constant teasing from her classmates. Of course, these things bothered her and she suffered from poor self-esteem. My parents tried hard to teach her not to let events at school affect her, but that was to no avail. At one time, Krystal tried her hand at extracurricular activities. She campaigned for student body president in fifth grade. She worked diligently on that campaign, and my heart went out to her because I saw firsthand her excitement and how much energy she put into it. I remember her walking into the house after school on the day of the election.

"How did you do?" I asked.

She smiled and said, "I lost," and immediately burst into tears and ran to her bedroom.

Krystal joined the band and played saxophone in sixth grade. She practiced for hours and hours; still, her hard work did not lead to her sitting first chair, or second chair, or third chair. She sat last chair and would do so throughout her junior high and high school years. By her own account, she "…was a terrible saxophone player." Her band teacher even made negative comments about her saxophone playing, and oftentimes her classmates laughed at her when she was called to play before the class.

A visit to the doctor at the age of 15 provided Krystal with the breakthrough she so desperately needed. Her doctor discovered she was severely hearing impaired. Within days, she was fitted with hearing aids for each ear, and from that day forward, her life changed forever. After receiving the hearing aids, Krystal began to achieve at a higher level in school. She improved her performance in band and even began taking piano lessons.

As a senior in high school, Krystal decided to participate in an annual solo and ensemble competition at Troy State University in Troy, Alabama. Much of the attention heading into the competition was focused on one of her classmates, the first chair saxophonist, who was going to play a piece by Mozart. The band teacher was thrilled that his first chair player was performing such a compelling piece. The band director did not say much to Krystal about her solo.

It was Krystal's piano teacher who helped her find a saxophone piece for the competition. After tremendous effort, made more effective because she could now hear, Krystal received a superior rating for her performance, as well as a medal, a tremendous victory for her.

In college, Krystal's struggles continued but were of a different sort. She wore hearing aids and used equipment in class that would allow her to hear her professors through a headset as they spoke into a clip-on microphone. However, it was not uncommon for one of her professors to say he would not wear the microphone. In fact, during her last semester in college where she majored in education and prepared for her teaching certification, one of her professors told her he would not wear that "thing." Krystal vowed to report him, but he responded with a resounding, "I don't care." Nevertheless, he did not wear the microphone and his lack of cooperation hurt Krystal immensely as she struggled in the course. She was still able to pass with a C.

Despite Krystal's challenges, she has had the courage to persist and not give up. Over the past decade, she has earned her Master's in Education, a specialist degree, and an administration degree in Education. She is currently pursuing her doctoral degree in education. She is a teacher in the Muscogee County School District in Columbus, Georgia, and most importantly, she is married and has two children. I love my sister. I admire her work ethic and her willingness to fight for what she believes. She has endured and overcome a lot. The only thing Krystal ever wanted was to be treated equally and respected for who she is and the work she does. Krystal has always been my biggest fan (and my biggest critic). Now, I am her biggest fan.

On the Surface…Beneath It All

According to **Merriam-Webster's** Online Dictionary, the word *hypocrisy* is defined as "feigning to be what one is not or to believe what one does not." One author defined hypocrisy as "the practice of professing beliefs, feelings, or virtues that one does not hold or possess; falseness."

In the book *The World's Most Powerful Leadership Principle*, Jim Hunter defines leadership as the "skill of influencing people to enthusiastically work toward goals identified as being for the common good." However, problems arise when hypocrisy and leadership are intertwined. Those who must follow this type of leader find themselves trying to survive in an environment of "don't blink; don't believe everything you hear; don't believe everything you see; and for gosh sakes, watch your back."

Noel Tipton was raised by his parents to be a hardworking young man. His work ethic afforded him the opportunity to play college athletics at State University, earn an MBA, get his foot in the door of a company in his hometown, and eventually rise to a senior-level manager. Noel is a member of the town's high society and trendy elite and is very involved in the community. He is frequently interviewed by the local media for supporting any charity that advocates youth or health issues. Noel's name is often the first to come up when a new civic or city board appointment is open. Noel does everything first class, from his shiny new company automobile and his house in the hills, to his expensively and artistically decorated office on the main floor of corporate headquarters. Noel looks good physically and he is well-spoken. He knows how to wow a crowd with a speech. A common remark about his character from those in the civic arena is, "He's such a nice, wonderful and fun guy. You couldn't ask for a better person to work with."

However, that is the public Noel Tipton. His employees feel differently. Among themselves they wonder how in the world community people could make such comments about Noel's great character. Most people in the community only see him for an hour or so each week. His employees, on the other hand, work with him every day and see a different side of Noel. To them Noel is a high-flying, unprincipled and unscrupulous division manager who is a incredibly "smooth operator." The people in the community are blinded to this side of Noel because they see only his public persona.

Noel's employees remember the time he promoted John to be his chief assistant. John did so well that he began to receive numerous accolades from people in the community and those in John's peer group outside the company. Noel became jealous of John and began to have John followed around town as he went from meeting to meeting. It was not long before Noel had John transferred to another department. Noel's employees also knew he fed them from a long-handled spoon and he kept pertinent and helpful information to himself. They knew how grumpy he could be. Even though they saw the hypocrisy, the employees chuckled when the "big boss" visited their department. They had never seen Noel's smile so bright. He told jokes and laughed at everything the big boss said. The employees looked on in amazement and wondered what work might be like if Noel were this pleasant all the time.

There is a lot to learn from Noel Tipton. He has a second-to-none work ethic and outside of work, a pleasing personality. Noel can also work a room with the best of them and he has a huge network of acquaintances from all over the country. However, these positives are overshadowed by his need to be the alpha male in his sphere of influence. He has worked extremely hard to get to where he is, and he is greatly admired by many. This "I am the head man in charge" attitude cancels his positive leadership characteristics. When he truly learns to trust those in his work environment and understands that the people he hired are not out to get him, when he works as hard to support those in his division at work as he does to impress those in the community, when his public personality matches his work personality, only then will he be known as a transcendent leader versus a manager who gets the job done.

Lost Art or Virtuous Ideal?

Have you cultivated the art of effective communication? Do you take pride in your ability to interact with the people in your sphere of influence? Are you available for your employees when they need you? Servant leaders understand the value of effective communication.

Being a servant leader requires the necessary communication skills in order to have influence with the people you've been entrusted to lead. In today's fast-paced (microwave-speed, I want it now) society, there are numerous ways to communicate with people. There is the "old" landline telephone; the new cell phone in various colors, shapes, and sizes; numerous instant messaging services, e-mail, and social networking sites such as Facebook and MySpace. But don't be fooled; nothing takes the place of good old-fashioned face-to-face contact.

In order to be an effective communicator, you must:

Be able to work with people. A good friend of mine, Jim, told me about a meeting he once had with his manager. The manager praised Jim for being the best leader in the division and for his ability to communicate effectively with his employees. He kindly thanked her for the words of encouragement. But then the manager said she did not particularly like working with people. If she had her way, Jim would be the one to talk to the employees on her behalf! By definition, *leadership* is the skill of influencing people. So, how can a person positively influence another human being if he or she does not enjoy being around them?

Stop the Houdini Act. One common complaint I hear from employees is the disrespect they feel when their manager leaves the office but doesn't tell them he or she is leaving. And sometimes the manager is gone for hours or even a full day. What if something comes up? What if the leader is needed? Personally, I find this to be insulting. I don't care where he or she is going.

That's not the issue. Managers should be considerate enough to communicate to their employees that they will be out of the office for a while.

Speak to people. Attention: all introverts, this message is for you. Studies show that 87 percent of a person's success is due to his people skills. It doesn't matter how many degrees he has or how technical his expertise. If you cannot communicate effectively with other people, then they will not want to work with you. Here is a news flash: If this is your Achilles heel, watch out! There is a major speed bump down the road.

Studies show that people in organizations typically spend 3/4 of their time in an interpersonal situation in the workplace. This statistic alone tells us why communication is so important. One cannot have a sphere of influence without people, and when it comes to influence, it is all about communicating well.

Communication is a skill that is just as important as technical skills, if not more so. In order to be effective, communication must be practiced often. Effective communication is the breeding ground for trust and respect, and it is essential to leading in the 21st century.

Who's Covering Your Front Desk?

During the Christmas holiday season, Americans spend a lot of time shopping and buying presents. I am curious to know whether you receive exceptional service when you enter the store of your choice.

As a customer, I know that some sales representatives are good with customers, and some are not. It is the leader's responsibility in any business to make sure the right employees are put in positions to succeed. From my experience as a manager, but more importantly as a customer, I can tell which stores spend time on customer service training and development, and which stores do not. Can't you?

I believe that for a business to be successful, it is vitally important for its leaders to place the right employee at the front desk. It is critical to entrust the most harmonious, engaging, verbal and extroverted employees out front with the customers. These are employees whose natural instincts are to want to be around people. Taking the time to get to know the customer is not a job to these people; it is a way of life. These employees have a smile on their face regardless of the situation. They are the gateway to the soul of your organization and they are usually the ones who leave people with a positive (or negative) overall impression about your place of business.

There are also employees you do not want at the front desk greeting customers. I am referring to people who, although cordial and nice, are reserved, distant and non-verbal. For the most part, they are downright disengaging. Being around people and meeting with customers eight hours a day is simply not what they enjoy doing. We have all seen these people sitting at the front desk or counter when we enter a particular establishment. They do not smile much. They look gloomy. If you ask them a question, you will never get more than a short answer. If you want conversation, forget about it. They are not interested, so don't bother. These people are not bad. On the contrary, they are just being asked to do something that is not a natural fit with their personality.

Case in point: Several years ago, my oldest daughter had an eye exam. When we returned to pick up her glasses a week later, the receptionist greeted us with a huge smile and asked our purpose for the visit. I told her. She was quite friendly and kidded me for wearing my Auburn University shirt (this was the day before the annual Auburn/Georgia football game), and after some light banter, she pointed us to one of the service tables and told us we were next. Moments later, another employee came over to the desk and told us loudly that we had to move. She said she had a customer and that we were not next and repeated that we needed to move. Her tone and her unfriendly nature were polar opposites of the receptionist who had greeted us. The same point could have been made with a different tone. I could have stayed to argue with her, but why waste energy? We left. My daughter eventually got her glasses (when my wife took her the next morning). In my estimation, this business lost three future customers and $400 to $500 in revenue in a span of 45 seconds. Everyone in my family wears glasses, but three of us will not be shopping at this particular store again. Sound familiar? Unfortunately this happens way too often.

It is the leader's responsibility to place people in the right positions to succeed. The leader must learn the personalities and character traits of his people. Placing people in the wrong jobs makes life miserable for everyone. I have a question for the leader and for the customer. If you are a leader, who is covering your front desk? If you're a customer, and you visit a place to spend your hard-earned money, are you satisfied with the service you receive?

Warts and All

I have been in the business world for nearly 20 years, and I have yet to meet a leader who is perfect. As much as I like reading biographies and watching documentaries of great leaders, I still have not studied one who is perfect. Do you know why? Because we are all human and the idea that any human is perfect is in and of itself an imperfect thought.

All leaders are imperfect to varying degrees. I cannot be Tiger Woods, Michael Jordan, or Dr. Martin Luther King, Jr. However, I *can* strive to be the best Kelvin Redd that I can possibly be, and believe me, the Kelvin Redd that I know is fraught with imperfections. That is why I love legendary basketball coach John Wooden's definition of *success*, which says, "Success is peace of mind which is a direct result of self-satisfaction in knowing you made the effort to become the best of which you are capable." This is known as continuous development. After all, is there any better goal than giving your best?

Does continuous development mean you will get better each and every day? I don't think so, but it does mean you are striving to be the best you can be. Let's face it, some days will be better than others. On some days you will feel as though you can do no wrong, and then there will be other days when it feels like the sky is falling down on you. In essence, those feelings are called *life*.

Becoming a servant leader is an evolutionary process. In fact, striving to be any type of leader is an evolutionary process. We may never get there, and as the "ole" folks used to say when I was a little boy, "I am not what I *want* to be, but thank God I am not what I *used* to be!"

You see, I eat and sleep servant leadership, and I am beginning to believe that we are placing our leaders on too high a pedestal. We expect too much of them. When the word *leader* comes to mind, there is a growing perception that a leader should do no wrong. There has only been one leader in my life that could do no wrong, and He departed this earth 2,000 years ago.

In closing, the next time you see your *leader*, look at him or her as being human first. He or she will make mistakes. Leadership is a skill, and everything I know about a skill is that it takes practice–lots and lots of practice (*if* you want to be really good). People do make mistakes, and if they live another day, they live to make another, and another, and maybe just one more. When someone you know signs on to be your leader, realize that you are getting not just a person, but their life experiences and what makes them who they are…"warts and all."

Giving Praise

Have you ever accomplished something you were extremely proud of, and you couldn't wait to share your good news with your friends and family? Obviously, you were extremely excited when you told them the news but in no way did you intend to be boastful or arrogant. However, to your disappointment and amazement, not everyone shared in your excitement. While some of them ignored you, others gave you the obligatory congratulations with a wry smile.

In one of my workshops, a participant, Michael, told the group he had received an award for bringing in the most accounts in his company. His immediate supervisor was happy for him and told him so, but it was the behavior of his division manager that caught Michael off guard since he thought they had a good relationship. They saw each other at weekly meetings and on occasion would sit together over coffee in the break room and discuss world events.

The division manager knew how hard Michael had worked to achieve the award, yet he never congratulated him. In fact, when the two gentlemen's paths crossed several times over the next week, the accomplishment was never mentioned. Although this didn't bother Michael to depths of despair, he did find the division manager's behavior rather odd.

Michael had seen the division manager make a fuss over other employees when they did well. He had to have known about the award because the announcement email distributed by corporate headquarters to the employees was sent to all managers first.

At an all-day corporate sales meeting two weeks later, Michael had the opportunity to sit next to his division manager. During one of the breaks, Michael asked him what he thought of Michael's award. He looked at Michael and gave him a smile, with a wrinkle and no emotion, and said he thought it was a great accomplishment. Nothing more and nothing less. End of discussion.

Michael was crushed. He had worked hard and was honored for it.

However, after he achieved the award, he simply wanted the people he saw every day to share in his excitement. His feelings were hurt and he questioned the division manager's motives. From then on, when the manager told the group how much he wanted his division to be the best and how much he cared for each individual, Michael had an hard time believing him.

In Bill Turner's 10 characteristics of a servant leader he says, "In a well-run servant leadership organization it is essential to recognize and celebrate both individual and group performance and achievements. A leader must be a cheerleader in bad times as well as good times."

Consciously withholding praise is not uncommon in a me-myself-and-I world. But this type of behavior is not just found in those who hold a formal leadership position. Family, friends and the people we see every day also practice this type of behavior.

Giving praise is important to the people we lead, but doing so without emotion decreases morale.

If your leader or the people close to you consciously withhold praise or commend you without emotion, do not let this stop you from trying as hard as you can. And do not, I repeat, *do not* apologize for your success. Be humble, yes, but not overly humble to the point that your humility is false. Continue striving to be the best you can be. A leader's poor behavior is a reflection of his character, not yours.

Servant Leadership Teams

"The strength of the pack is the wolf, and the strength of the wolf is the pack." – Kipling

According to Chris Stowell, Vice President of International Business Development for the Center for Management and Organization Effectiveness, "A team is a tight-knit group of competent individuals who care deeply about each other. They are fiercely committed to their mission, and are highly motivated to combining their energy and expertise to achieve a common objective." Legendary football coach Vince Lombardi once said, "Individual commitment to a group effort— that is what makes a team work, a company work, a society work, a civilization work."

As far back as I can remember I have been a part of some tremendous teams. It started with my father, James B. Redd. For 14 years, he was the head basketball coach at Central High School in Phenix City, Alabama. He won more than 400 games. His 1981 team won 33 consecutive games and was ranked number one in the state for most of the 1980-81 season. More importantly, in 14 years of coaching, 50 of his players received college scholarships.

Although I was a part of several teams, not all of the successful teams I was a part of have been sports-related. When I was a freshman in high school, our symphonic band placed first in the state. For 13 years I worked for Synovus Financial Corp. in Columbus, Georgia, a company rated by *Fortune* magazine in 1999 as the Best Place to Work in America. For the past three years, I have been the Associate Director and Director at the Center for Servant Leadership at the Pastoral Institute in Columbus, Georgia. The PI, as we affectionately call it, has been consistently recognized as the best Samaritan Center in the country.

All of these successful teams have common characteristics:

Exceptional leadership. The leadership of each of the above mentioned organizations worked hard at being leaders. They led with integrity, honesty, care and humility. As John Maxwell says, "Everything begins and ends with leadership."

Shared vision. In Peter Senge's *Fifth Discipline*, a shared vision is the mechanism used for building shared meaning. It is the organization's "deep purpose that expresses the organization's reason for existence." It's not enough for the leadership to know where the organization is going. Every team member must know the team's vision.

Overcome adversity. Let's face it, all teams face adversity. My father's last team to make it to the state tournament had to overcome a 20-point second quarter deficit to win the regional finals in order to get to the state tournament. The successful teams are survivors. When the going gets tough, they get tougher. In short, they rise to the occasion.

Dedicated team members. Each member enjoyed being a part of the team. As former University of North Carolina head basketball coach Dean Smiths said, they "worked hard, they worked smart, and they worked together." The team members felt strongly that they were growing as persons.

Disciplined environment. It was fun being a part of these organizations, and I absolutely love working for the Pastoral Institute right now. However, successful teams cannot have fun unless the organization is grounded in discipline.

Servant leadership team members know their roles and perform them with competence. Thus, they are highly self-aware. Servant leadership teams have a high degree of caring and trust. Successful teams are not developed overnight. They take time, patience and hard work. Successful teams are made up of team members who will go to great lengths for their leaders, their organization and their fellow team members.

Three Simple Steps: How to Create a Departmental Servant Leadership Program

Are you a department or division manager or school principal? Do you work for a large organization that has many moving parts? Have you ever wished for a servant leadership movement within your organization? Have you ever wanted to start a servant leadership program of your own but you just didn't know quite how or where to begin? If you answered yes to these questions, you're in luck because the Center for Servant Leadership has developed three simple steps to implementing and maintaining a servant leadership program within your very own department, division or school. And just think, after a short period of time, your department will be known as the "Best Department to Work For" in your organization.

Step One: Know the Philosophy

By definition, servant leadership is a lifelong journey that includes the discovery of one's self, a desire to serve others and a commitment to lead. Thus, departmental training is essential. It is an awesome gift and privilege to be a leader and it shouldn't be taken lightly. Everyone in the department should be provided valuable training in the basic knowledge of the philosophy of servant leadership. Bestselling author Jim Hunter says that "leadership is the skill of influence." The values of servant leadership can be learned and applied by all employees who have the desire to effect real change, and to advance, develop and transform the department into becoming a great place to work.

Step Two: Know Yourself

Servant leaders are often considering questions such as: Who am I? Why am I here? What makes me unique? Are my actions enabling others to grow as individuals? Are my actions motivated by honesty and love?

However, as writer and management consultant Peter Drucker points out, "Most Americans do not know what their strengths are. When you ask them, they look at you with a blank stare, or they respond in terms of subject knowledge, which is the wrong answer." In the book, *First Break All the Rules*, Marcus Buckingham says of great managers, "When motivating someone, they *focus on strengths*... not on weaknesses." He later says, "Each person's pattern of talents is enduring, resistant to change."

As Bill Turner says, "A person cannot be an effective leader, if he/she doesn't know who he/she is." Where do your talents lie? What do you enjoy doing? Do you know your strengths? Dr. Geil Browning, founder of Emergenetics International, says, "Your thinking and behavioral preferences are your strengths. They make all the difference in how you think, behave, and communicate. Go with them and you'll be more satisfied and more productive...Being in alignment with yourself at work will make you more effective... Working against your innate preferences will tire you out...Using a Whole Emergenetics approach, you will be more successful at bringing people together. This in turn, will help you be a stronger leader." A person on the journey to servant leadership should be intentional about his or her own self-development. According to Bill George in his book *True North*, when the 75 members of the Stanford Graduate School of Business Advisory Council were asked to recommend the most important capability for leaders to develop, their answer was nearly unanimous: self-awareness.

Step Three: Know It Forever

Here is your opportunity to effect real and lasting change within your department. As your department's journey toward servant leadership continues, everyone now has knowledge of the servant leadership philosophy and a better understanding of themselves (but remember, it's still a journey).

Individual and group meetings are the perfect way to maintain and grow your department. And there is no better way to do this than by performing *servant leadership coaching*. Also known by a variety of titles, including professional coaching, executive coaching, and life coaching among others, it has emerged as a powerful force and resource for helping individuals realize their fullest potential. Coaching is being utilized extensively in departments all across the corporate world. Coaching for some is becoming highly specialized in a variety of corporate settings; yet, the basic issues related to coaching are incorporated in understanding the concepts of servant leadership coaching. Coaching is about empowering the other person and enabling the department to discover and fulfill their goals and dreams. Coaching is committed to helping others become self-fulfilled in their work and their life. It is leading others to discover their fullest potential and live this out daily.

There you have it—three simple steps to implementing your own departmental servant leadership program. The philosophy is ageless, everlasting and unchanging. There is no better leadership philosophy in the world that will help you confront the leadership challenges of the 21st Century.

Good Luck!

Know Your Mission

Do you know your life's mission? I do. That is why I try to keep from getting overwhelmed by things that are unimportant to my purpose. As I have matured, I understand that it is okay to say no. I have also learned how to prevent the bad experiences I had in the past as a result of not saying no. Not spreading myself too thin is vitally important to me.

It is so easy to get bogged down in things that are not important to your life's mission, whether at work or at home. We often put too much focus on the "energy drainers," things that keep us from doing what's important in life. We make our Things to Do Lists, and as long as things are checked off, we feel a sense of accomplishment. But it is important not to mistake activity for achievement.

Personally, I wrestle with spreading myself too thin. I saw this happen to my father, and I promised myself long ago that I would not travel down that same road. Whenever I feel I need a break, I will take one. I cannot do the work I'm supposed to do if I don't have the time, or the energy, to do it.

I take my responsibility as a "family man" seriously. I have been married for 16 years, and don't let anyone fool you, being married is hard work. You get out of marriage what you put into it, so I try especially hard to meet the needs of my wife. We have also been blessed with two wonderful daughters, and they have interests, too (inside and outside of the home). I must make myself available for guitar, dance, swimming, and tennis lessons. I take pride in knowing I have made it to about 95 percent of their school and extracurricular activities.

I work full-time. I am an adjunct instructor, and I am also involved in several civic organizations. I am fortunate that I get the chance to meet lots of people in my line of work, and I am very passionate about what I do. However, recently I had to re-evaluate how I spent my time. I found myself becoming too emotionally drained to do the things that are important to my life's mission. That is why I have started to examine what things, outside of family and work, are important.

Saying no is an important aspect of not spreading yourself too thin. I learned this the hard way. There was a time in my life when I found it hard to say no, and the results were not good.

Several years ago, I was asked to join a civic organization, and I did. Shortly thereafter, I was asked to become the organization's president. I said yes, and that was a big mistake. At that time in my life, I was in school and was in the midst of a career change, and I had an awful lot on my mind. I should not have joined the organization, let alone accepted the presidency. It was a total disaster because my heart was not in it, not in the least bit. As a result, the progress of the organization suffered. My attitude turned sour and then my relationships suffered. I was not an effective president and other responsibilities were impacted.

It is important to maintain your focus. Make time for family and significant other people. Be mindful and compassionate when saying no to those who want your time. Take time for you and do not waste time on things that are not important to your mission.

Embracing Pressure: The Final Exam

According to Viara Gurova and Vanya Bozhilova, "Usually people speak about pressure and stress in a negative way, but to be under pressure has some advantages: people become more organized; concentrate more; do more in less time; generate good ideas; neglect unimportant things. You should see pressure as a challenge and opportunity for proving yourself." These advantages were never more evident in my life than during my last semester of college.

All the years of school were finally coming to an end. I had one term remaining before graduating. I could not believe it. In a sense, it had sneaked up on me. In that last month, I called the Bursar's Office three times to make sure I was indeed going to graduate.

As most parents would be, my parents were extremely excited about my forthcoming graduation day. They valued education so highly. My graduation was particularly important to my father because he had fallen ill, so I desperately wanted to see a smile on his face on graduation day.

I needed 18 hours to complete my degree, which meant I had to take four classes during my final semester. I did not want the classes to be too challenging, but three of the four would be. Luckily, one of my classes would be an elective, so I decided to take something fun, like a speech class. After all, the previous two speech classes I had taken were easy.

This class was different. Prior to the mid-term exam I had made C's on my first five speeches. I was in total disbelief. To further complicate matters, I failed the mid-term exam terribly.

I was literally scared to death. Everyone in my family was looking to me, the first Redd of my generation and the second member of my family (my father being the first) to graduate college. The pressure was building, and I continued making C's on my speeches!

Soon, finals approached. I not only had to pass the exam, but I also pretty much had to ace it. The only hope I had was to work as hard and as smart as I possibly could, and that is exactly what I did. I studied as hard as I have for any other class before or since that three-hour course. I literally ignored my other three classes and put all of my efforts into the speech class.

Finally, exam day arrived. I was confident, and my preparation showed. I made a 94 on the final exam, and it counted double. I earned a C in the class. My final semester grades as an undergraduate student: two A's, one B, and one C.

What did I learn from my final exam experience? For starters, I learned to not count my chickens before they hatch. I thought the speech class was going to be easy and that I would not have to work very hard. I also learned how to work under pressure and not run from it. I realized that there will be many times in my life when I will be tested, but if I embrace the pressure, it will bring out the best in me.

Leading in Tough Times

"Nothing in the world can take the place of persistence. Talent will not; nothing is more common than unsuccessful men with talent. Genius will not; unrewarded genius is almost a proverb. Education will not. The world is full of educated derelicts. Persistence and determination alone are omnipotent. The slogan, 'Press on,' has solved and always will solve the problems of the human race."
- Calvin Coolidge

We all have our tough times. For some people, a tough time is trying to make both ends meet and put food on the table or trying to find transportation to work. Tough times in the workplace can mean many different things. It may be dealing with a difficult work environment, trying to pass a test, poor sales results or a challenging project. It doesn't always help matters when you watch the news channels. Lately the airwaves have been saturated with negativity. From the wars in Iraq and Afghanistan, to the rising cost of gasoline, to the poor state of our economy. This is the situation in which we find ourselves. However, how you handle your tough times says a lot about the outcome you will have.

The following are eight ways to lead yourself and your employees through tough times:

> *Acknowledge the situation.* The first thing you must do is acknowledge the situation at hand. Don't run from it and don't play the blame game. When you start blaming your competitors or the economy or whatever, you are giving yourself and your employees an unrealistic way out. Ok, so your sales are down. What are you going to do about it? Having problems passing the test? What are you going to do about it?

Hold the Vision. Former Chairman and CEO of General Electric, Jack Welch, once said, "Good business leaders create a vision, articulate the vision, passionately own the vision, and relentlessly drive it to completion." Obviously, you do not want to overreact, but this is not the time to be passive. When the going gets tough, the leader holds the vision.

Have Courage. In the book *A Leader's Legacy*, authors Kouzes and Posner say, "Courage is about making tough choices, but those choices more often than not involve the little things we do. Do I say yes or do I say no? Do I stay or do I leave? Do I speak or do I stay silent? None of these choices on the surface feels particularly frightening, but in the proper context they can be terrifyingly difficult. It's not for anyone else to decide whether someone's act is courageous or not. Ultimately what takes courage and what does not is a very personal decision."

Know Yourself. Do you have the skills to do the job that you have been entrusted to do? It is far easier to manage a situation when you have the capacity do so. It is when you do not have the talent for a job that the situation can become very challenging. Any coach in any sport in America will tell you that you cannot win without talent.

Listen. Seek wise counsel and listen to them. There are people in your midst who can help you. However, sometimes it is hard to listen to someone when your mind is in a fog. Who are the people you are listening to?

Teamwork. There is a high probability that you cannot make it through your tough times alone. Surround yourself with good people—people who have your best interests at heart. My favorite verse in the Bible is Proverbs 13:20 which says, "He who walks with wise men shall be wise but a companion of fools shall be destroyed." Who are your wise men?

Think Positive. It is never a good time to have a pity party. Try your best to avoid anything and everything that places you in a negative state of mind. One local executive even told me that he doesn't watch the news because of what "it" does to him.

Remain Calm. Be still. There is nothing worse than a leader who runs around shouting, "The sky is falling! The sky is falling!" Your calmness may instill confidence and clearer thinking in all those working toward a solution.

How you lead through the current state of the world is significant. In order to be well positioned for the future, you first have to get through the present. Weathering tough times requires a keen sense of what obstacles and opportunities lay ahead. I hope these key points to leading in tough times are helpful.

My Name Is John and I'm an Introvert...

So Please Remember Me and My Friends When You Plan This Year's After-hours Christmas Party

Hello, my name is John and I am an introvert. There have been many myths associated with the definitions of introvert/extrovert, so before I go any further, I want to make sure you understand the definition.

The definitions of an introvert/extrovert can best be summed up by a question, and that question is: Where do you get your energy from? Introverts get their energy from being alone while extroverts get their energy from being with other people. Remember, the key word in this definition is energy and according to Dr. Ed Diener from the University of Illinois, "Extroverts make up 60 to 70 percent of society and introverts account for 20 to 30 percent."

My extroverted friend thinks I don't like people. That cannot be further from the truth. I love people. I love being around people, just not 24/7 like him.

I do not have a full after-work schedule like my extroverted friend, either. On Monday, my friend gets together with his other extroverted friends to watch Monday Night Football. Tuesdays are reserved for coaching his little league football team (basketball in the winter and baseball in the summer). Wednesday night is church night, and he attends an after-hours business social on Thursday. When I see him during the week, all he talks about is how he cannot wait for the weekend to get here so he can go canoeing or mountain climbing with his travel club. No, we introverts have to draw the line somewhere. Even that famous/busy man who lived 2,000 years ago had to escape to the mountains to get away from it all every now and then.

I think you should know that I am around people all day long, every day of the week. I love being in sales, and I love meeting new people. Last year I was my division's top salesperson. That's right.

Introverts can be outstanding salespeople. Remember, it is all about the "energy." That is why I guard mine so dearly. I have to plan well so I do not waste my reserves.

If I have a full week of sales presentations, promotions, events and meetings, Friday nights are usually spent relaxing. I may go out to dinner with one or two friends, but I am comforted knowing it is Friday, and the weekend belongs to me. For me, there is nothing better than being in control of my Saturday and Sunday schedule.

My extroverted friend does not understand me at all. For instance, one day we were talking and he said he could not believe I was an introvert. He said, "How can you be an introvert? You told me you attend football games every Saturday, and I know there must be at least 85,000 people in that stadium." I responded by telling him I do not speak to every one of those people and that I usually just converse with the two or three people in my section who, by the way, I have known for years. Being part of a crowd is okay with me. You will never see me behave like my extroverted friend, though. When he enters a crowded room, he makes it a point to try to speak to everyone. When I enter that same room, I try to find someone I know and hold court with him. I guess you could say that the major difference between my extroverted friend and me is this: After being around people all day long, at the end of the day, I would rather go home, recline and relax whereas my extroverted friend would rather meet friends.

Being self-aware is an important aspect of servant leadership. Only after understanding yourself can you gain full knowledge of understanding others, so when you extroverts out there begin planning this year's after-hours office Christmas party, particularly on a Friday night (Heaven forbid on a Saturday night), just remember that while half the people at the party are thinking of the event as fun, the other half may be thinking of the party as an extended workday.

Share Your Vision

Several years ago I gave a speech to the Columbus State University Servant Leadership students at their monthly Reflections lunch. There were about 40 people in attendance. Mr. Bill Turner was also present in the audience. The topic of my speech was Define Your Destiny. I talked to the students about the importance of having desire, investing in their talents, and having a strong and positive vision of themselves.

There was time left for questions and answers at the conclusion of my speech. One young man stood up and asked, "What's your vision?"

"I can't tell you that," I promptly responded.

"Why not?" he asked.

"Because where I come from you don't tell anybody else your dreams," I retorted with a hint of cynicism.

He was beginning to invade my territory I thought to myself. Just as I made that statement I saw Mr. Turner out of the corner of my eye. He looked like he was about to raise his hand but he slowly put it back down. When I finished my speech and Q&A was over, I went to my seat. Ironically, my seat was next to Mr. Turner.

As I took a sip of water, Mr. Turner looked at me and said, "I started to ask you a question."

"What was it?" I asked.

"Why didn't you answer that young man's question about sharing your vision?" he inquired.

"Mr. Turner, that's just not something I was brought up doing. I didn't feel comfortable telling him my vision," I said (with all due respect).

He looked at me in what was one of those freeze-framed moments. "Kelvin, I'd be willing to believe that people would be more apt to help you than hurt you if you shared your vision." *Whoa!* I thought. There was a long pause—maybe a second or two but it seemed longer.

"I wish you hadn't said that," I groaned.

"Why not?" he said inquisitively.

"Because you've just ruined the rest of my day," I said with a laugh.

"Well, I don't want to do that," he said with a look of bewilderment.

"No, sir. Don't get me wrong. It's just that I'm probably going to be thinking about this conversation all afternoon," I said.

We both laughed.

When I drove back to the office, I couldn't stop thinking about Mr. Turner's earlier comment to me.

Suddenly, as I turned into the Pastoral Institute's parking lot, it hit me (and like a ton of bricks).

A loud voice spoke to me, 'What would have happened if Jesus Christ had not shared his vision with the world? Where would this world be right now?'

And right there at the moment, I made a conscious choice on this lifelong journey of mine to share my vision with anyone who inquired.

A visionary is a person who is courageous, inspiring, and imaginative; and you don't have to be famous to be one. Interestingly enough, most people don't become famous until after they share their vision. Wow! What a paradox. The vision may not necessarily be for the person who was inspired by the vision. In many cases, the beneficiary of the vision is someone else. Don't be afraid to share your vision. Anyone with vision can accomplish great things.

Regaining Your Swing

Have you ever been asked to perform a task or something you were once very good at? Have you ever had to take the lead on a project, sing a solo in the church choir or conduct a presentation before your management group? And while preparing for such a task, did you experience negative thoughts that said you were incapable of performing the task? Have any of these things ever happened to you?

When a person feels he cannot perform the way in which he is accustomed, it is not unusual for that person to conduct himself in a manner that is contrary to who he really is. This oftentimes leads to *bad thinking.* This type of thinking says things like, "I'm not good enough... People are out to get me...I don't trust them...They don't like me anyway...I can't count on anyone but myself...or, Who cares?

Our daily lives are filled with experiences that can have a negative impact on our self-confidence, and in today's what-have-you-done-for-me-lately world, lacking self- confidence can halt any desires or dreams of achievement. For many people, the pressure to succeed can be enormous.

One of my favorite movies is *The Legend of Bagger Vance,* which illustrates this point. The story takes place in Savannah, Georgia in the 1930s. The main character was Rannulph Junuh, and he had it all. He was a handsome, up-and-coming champion golfer, and he was in love with the daughter of one of the town's wealthiest men.

However, Junuh's life took a dramatic turn when he was called into action to fight in World War I. When he returned from the war, Junuh was despondent and turned to alcohol and gambling to soothe the spirits that haunted him. He lost confidence in himself and nearly everything else. (As my daughter would say, Junuh was a "hot mess.")

Later, Junuh's former socialite girlfriend was on the verge of losing her late father's ostentatious golf club resort. Although he resisted, she ultimately persuaded Junuh to participate in an exhibition golf tournament to help save the club. She'd already lined up two legendary world champion golfers, Walter Hagen and Bobby Jones, to take part in the tournament.

With his confidence shattered, Junuh was terrified. The mere thought of being on the same golf course with Hagen and Jones was overwhelming.

One evening, Junuh was in his backyard practicing hitting golf balls. He was errant one shot after another and was frustrated because this was something he used to be more than capable of doing. Suddenly, a stranger appeared. It was Bagger Vance.

Bagger said to Junuh, "I hear you lost your swing. I guess we got to find it. See, the trick is…to find your swing…"

"What'd you say?" responded Junuh.

"Well, you lost your swing. We got to find it…Now it's somewhere… in the harmony of all that is, all that was, and all that will be…" says Bagger.

Regaining self-confidence takes time and introspection. If you've lost your confidence, I suggest the following: First, speak positively to and about yourself. Tell yourself you 'can' rather than you 'cannot.' Second, surround yourself with the right people. When you are down, you need people who have your best interests at heart. Third, invest in your talents by focusing on your strengths and the things you do well. Finally, have faith. Know that you were put on this earth for a reason. God gave you something He gave no other, and He wants you to use it. But it's somewhere in the harmony of all that is, all that was and all that will be.

Don't Take Your Talent(s) for Granted

I have always enjoyed public speaking. It is what I am most passionate about. It is an extremely rare occasion when I am indifferent about conducting a speech. My mother has always told me that I have a talent for public speaking and that I should do it whenever called upon to do so. However, several years ago I wondered if my speaking career was in jeopardy.

I love Thanksgiving. It's my favorite holiday of the year. But in 2005, Thanksgiving Day was awful.

The whole family had gathered at my parents' home for Thanksgiving. I had just finished eating my dinner when I felt and heard a "pop" in my left temple. The sound was terrifying and the pain was excruciating. I decided to lie down for a while and see if it would go away. An hour elapsed, and the pain was still there, so my wife rushed me to the hospital. And that's where I spent the rest of Thanksgiving Day and night.

But that wasn't the end of it. The pain didn't go away. Between Thanksgiving Day and the first of the year, I had numerous doctor visits. Initially, I was diagnosed with having an ear infection. I knew that wasn't right. I had tubes placed in my ears three times between the ages of 4 and 18, so I grew up with ear infections. And this didn't feel like any ear infection I'd ever had.

Having a severe pain in the head and going several weeks without knowing its source was frightening. I'd never experienced a headache like this before. One night the pain was so severe I literally thought I was going to meet my Maker.

Finally, I was diagnosed with a TMJ (temporomandibular joint) problem. According to the American Academy of Otolaryngology, "TMJ is the joint where the mandible (the lower jaw) joins the temporal bone of the skull, immediately in front of the ear on each side of your head. A small disc of cartilage separates the bones, much like in the knee joint, so that the mandible may slide easily; each time you chew you move it." For a person like me who likes to talk a lot, a TMJ problem is Kryptonite.

After receiving the correct diagnosis, I thought to myself: *What if I won't be able to speak again?* What a terrible feeling that was. For as long as I can remember, I have always enjoyed public speaking. I'm not a tennis player, a golfer, or an attorney, and I am certainly not an underwriter. I am a speaker—pure and simple. Public speaking is what I do. It comes naturally to me, and I take it seriously.

The serious way I feel about public speaking was heightened several years ago after I conducted a keynote speech at a youth awards ceremony for a local civic organization. I gave what I thought was a good speech. But a couple of weeks later, I found out that one of the boys in the audience at the time committed suicide.

I was devastated. *If I'd only known he was having problems*, I thought, *perhaps I could have said something that night that would have made a difference in his life.* From that moment on, I've had a heightened level of consciousness about helping someone when I give a speech or present a workshop. That is why before every speech or workshop I say the following prayer: "God, please speak through me, act through me, and think through me."

The pain associated with the TMJ has disappeared. I'm in a good place now, and I'm having the best time of my life. I waited a long time to be where I am. When I think back to those months of suffering and distress, I realize how blessed I am that the correct diagnosis was made and that I am doing well now. I am extremely conscious of what I enjoy doing, and I take great pride in it. I encourage you—don't take your talents for granted. They can be taken away from you at any moment. So, when called upon to use your talents, do so with great preparation, humility, and joy!

Detours: Life's Blessings in Disguise

Dr. John Izzo, author of the book *Second Innocence: Rediscovering Joy and Wonder,* says, "The best things in life are not in your day-timer and probably weren't on your ten-year goal list. Although we make plans incessantly, many of the things we look back on with fondness were never in the grand game plan of our life. Our lives often unfold in a myriad of ways that were never part of our well-laid plans. If we are to experience a second innocence in our lives, to reconnect with the joy and wonder of life, we must begin to rethink how we see detours, the inevitable forks in the road that life gives us. Our commitment to our plans can blind us to the very path our soul wants to take us."

When I stop to think about it, my whole adult life has been filled with one detour after another. And thank goodness I followed them! For instance, a month before I was about to graduate from college, I was eagerly looking for a job in the Columbus, Georgia-Phenix City, Alabama area. My mother was in the grocery store and just happened to see a family friend. This friend told her that Total System Services, Inc. (now TSYS) was looking for employees for its Management Associate Program. Within two months after the application and interview process, the company hired me.

The most important detour in my life came when I met my wife, Faye. She was from Fort Mitchell, Alabama, which is just down the road from Phenix City. Oddly enough, the only time I had ever been to her hometown was when I was in the seventh grade and my junior high school basketball team, South Girard, played a game against Mt. Olive Junior High School of Fort Mitchell. Who knew that nearby town would hold my soul-mate? Nevertheless, one day when I came home from work, my sister said, "Kelvin, you've got to meet this girl." We went on a blind date that has led to 16 wonderful years of marriage and two beautiful daughters.

During my first year at TSYS, I was eagerly anticipating working in the client relations area. Instead, I was asked to create the company's first safety program. People laughed at me. Some people called me "Fire Marshall Bill." It was the last job I wanted to do, but as fate would have it, I learned more from that job than any other. I had a phenomenal manager who basically gave me a crash course MBA. I was continuously exposed to upper-level management. I was afforded the opportunity to travel the U.S. and abroad. I was promoted to assistant vice president and eventually managed the safety program for the Synovus Family of Companies.

Now I work at the Pastoral Institute in Columbus, Georgia. If someone had told me five years ago that I would work at the PI (that's what we call it), I would not have believed them. Not that there is anything wrong with the PI. On the contrary, it's a great place to work; it simply was not on my radar screen. I can sincerely say that I am truly having the best time of my professional career. This is the first job I have ever had where I don't feel as though I have to manufacture happiness.

I've always had a vision of what I wanted out of life. I'm a planner. I try my best to stay organized and know where I am going at all times. But as you can see, I've had detours and they've led to some great places and events. What about you?

The Mentor

I had been in the company nearly six months before we first met. He walked into the officers' meeting, waved and spoke to a couple of people in the room. After all these years, I found him most interesting at that particular moment. He was casual and polite but he didn't stand out. I just happened to notice him that morning, but there was something innately different about this man. In a few weeks, I would find out exactly what that was.

His name was Lynn Drury, and after I had spent nearly six months in the client relations area, I was to begin reporting to him. For a little more than a year, he would be my mentor, manager and friend.

Corporate America was not in my scope when I graduated college. I was a history major, so I was quite "green" when I arrived at Lynn's office for our first official meeting. His was the last office on a long hallway in the corporate headquarters.

When I arrived at his office, Lynn rose from his chair and greeted me with a handshake and a warm smile. For the next 50 minutes, he told me a quick version of his life's story. He told how and why he left one of the top Fortune 500 companies in the country and that he was glad to be home in Columbus, Georgia.

At the conclusion of our first meeting, I shook his hand and proceeded to leave the building through the exit door just outside of his office. I wasn't gone three seconds before I heard a knock on his window. Lynn motioned for me to come back into the building. When I re-entered, he said, "If I'm going to be your mentor, I need to tell you something. You're in corporate headquarters now, and you need to be seen. From now on, make sure you enter and exit this building through the front door in the lobby and not through the back exit."

Wow! I thought to myself. That made such a strong impression on me. The advice was so simple that it blew me away.

Lynn was an excellent communicator. Our offices were not in the same building, so he made sure the two of us met twice a week. He told me everything I needed to know about the company. Sometimes our meetings would run long, particularly when sharing our passion for reading. Whenever I called him and he wasn't in, he returned my phone call in a timely manner. This is something I valued, always appreciated and looked for in future managers.

I always thought Lynn would have made a great college professor. He was such a tremendous teacher, and I learned so much from him. Lynn taught me the importance of productivity and its relationship to units of output per employee hour, communication at all levels within an organization, planning well, being organized and finishing assignments on time. He even taught me how and what to order during a business lunch. While having lunch one day, he surprised me by demonstrating how to string a tea bag with a spoon.

We didn't "kumbaya" all of the time. Lynn was a tough manager, and whenever I did something he thought was unbecoming in a manager, he was quick to let me know about it.

Sadly, Lynn is no longer with us. He passed away a couple of years ago. No one has played a bigger role in my professional development than he did. Lynn was the ultimate mentor—demanding and confident, yet patient and kind. I owe him so much.

Facing Your Giants

Have you ever had the feeling that your life was spiraling out of control? That everything you did was not quite good enough? The attitude of the people surrounding you was no better than yours? And to top it all off, the one person you thought you could count on—that one person who always told you he had your back—appeared to be against you?

The movie *Facing the Giants* has numerous subplots, but I want to focus on the leadership of Grant Taylor, head football coach of Shiloh Christian Academy. Grant is portrayed as one of the nicest guys you could ever meet, but he is faced with many problems. First, he and his wife cannot have children and want them. Second, Grant has never had a winning football season as Shiloh's football coach. Third, he has a car, the only one he and his wife can afford, that is old and constantly breaks down. Finally, after beginning the football season with three straight losses, many of the parents want Grant fired. Matters are made worse when it appears that his assistant coach, who happens to be a friend, is in cahoots with the parents who want to get rid of Grant.

With all of these problems, it is easy to see why during the week of the school's fourth football game, Grant reaches a breaking point. He has no one to turn to and begins to question himself and his abilities. In one scene, he says to his wife, "I have been trying so hard. Why is life so unfair?" It is at this point, that his faith is tested, but it is also at this point that Grant relies on his faith to see him through this difficult period in his life.

He didn't lose confidence in himself. No longer was Grant paralyzed with fear. He grounded himself and his team in his beliefs. Grant asked the team to make a commitment, to give their best effort, not just on the football field but in life. Grant also asked his assistant coach to "get off the fence" and choose a side. His assistant coach chose to be on Grant's side. After a week of intense prayer, reflection, and introspection, the team won its first game of the year and every game after that on its way to a state championship. The players' grades even improved and so did their relationships.

The team's turnaround, and Grant's turnaround for that matter, wasn't about X's and O's. The turnaround was about a leader's realization that in order for his team to achieve the heights of which it was capable, his team needed a belief system that was grounded in trustworthiness, self-awareness, humility, caring, vision, empowerment, competence, good stewardship and community building. The team needed servant leadership.

By definition, servant leadership is a lifelong journey that includes discovery of one's self, a desire to serve others and a commitment to lead. No one ever said that our journey here on earth was going to be easy. On the contrary, at one time or another, each of us will be faced with giants in our lives. The questions Grant Taylor had about his role as a husband, football coach and human being are the same questions that servant leaders are often considering. They are: Who am I? Why am I here? What makes me unique? Are my actions enabling others to grow as individuals? Are my actions motivated by honesty and love?

I am a true believer in servant leadership. Life is not always going to be a bed of roses. I believe that if you want real success in your organization (or company, department, family, community), you must have a philosophy that its members can firmly rely on when the message of misery visits its bedside.

In conclusion, does your organization have a leadership philosophy? Do your constituents know your organization's leadership philosophy? Do your constituents believe in your organization's leadership philosophy? Do you believe in your organization's leadership philosophy?

Define Your Destiny

Dear Graduates,

Congratulations! This is a major accomplishment. You're a graduating senior. I am so proud of you. Enjoy the moment (within reason). However, keep in mind, this is only the beginning. The world awaits you. The world needs you. It needs your energy, your imagination, your intelligence, your poise, and your exuberance. But most of all, the world needs your leadership. Are you ready? I sure hope so. Just in case, and in order to help you along the way, I am giving you six steps to help you Define Your Destiny. They are:

Create a Burning Desire. In order to accomplish your goals in life, you must have desire. Napoleon Hill, an early twentieth century author and speaker, wrote, "Desire is step one to all achievement, not a wish, not a want, but a keen pulsating desire." So, whatever it is you want out of life, I have one question for you: How badly do you want it?

Enlarge Your Vision. Where do you see yourself a year from now? What about three years from now? You are not too young to have a true vision of your future. History is filled with people who have achieved greatness (notice I said greatness and not success – there are lots of people who are successful but not great) and who had a strong vision of themselves at a young age.

Discover Your Talent. You are a special person. You have been given a special gift. It's called a talent. Once you discover what it is, your life and the lives of people you touch will never be the same again. I once heard a speaker say, "Your talent is a gift to you from God. What you do with that talent is your gift back to Him." In short, don't just discover your talent – USE IT!

Establish Good Relationships. It's all about relationships, so make sure you surround yourself with people who want the best for you. One of my favorite sayings is, "Birds of a feather flock together." You can say a lot of things about Kelvin Redd, but you can never say that I hung around with the wrong crowd. If you're one of those individuals who has a tough time trying to find good people to hang around with, keep searching. They're out there.

Be Conscious of Life's Detours. Life has a way of throwing us a curve ball every now and then, and these curve balls can be real sinkers. Our biggest lessons in life sometimes occur when we are in the depths of the abyss. Just because you strike out and lose the ballgame doesn't mean that the season is over. But remember, detours are often life's blessings in disguise.

Shake the dirt off your shoulders. If you're over the age of 30, you may not know what this means. Luckily, I have a teenage daughter, so I know. In other words, not everyone is going to like you. I know this statement may shock you, but it is true and it has been this way since the dawn of time. In some form or fashion, we all want to be liked. However, in this world, you can't please everybody. So, as Jay Z says, "Shake the Dirt off Your Shoulders," and move on.

Best wishes,
Kelvin A. Redd

Present Moments of Thanksgiving

In *Life Transfigured: A Journal of Orthodox Nuns,* an anonymous author writes, "The spirit of thankfulness is a necessary part of the spiritual discipline of living in the present moment—with God—and not in the past or the future."

I experienced such a "present moment" a couple of years ago when I spent Thanksgiving Day with my wife's family. My wife's grandmother, Ms. Leola Owens, had recently turned 100 years old, so the family decided to invite everyone—and I do mean everyone— "back home" for Thanksgiving dinner.

Folks came from all over. There were dozens of family members and friends in attendance that day at Ms. Leola's farm in Macon County, Alabama. There were people from as far away as Florida, Ohio, and upstate New York.

My family and I arrived about an hour or so before dinner. It seemed as though everyone in attendance had someone to relate to. It was neat watching the great-grandkids and great-great-grandkids playing with one another. Some went horseback riding, while others fished in the pond or played ball. I spent time talking to some of the men folk and watching the afternoon football game.

When it was time for dinner, we all gathered around in a gigantic circle, held hands, and expressed what we were thankful for. It was amazing to hear generation after generation express their thankfulness and love for Ms. Leola and the family. What was equally amazing and even more of a blessing was seeing 70- and 80-year-old men and women use the word "Momma" as they spoke of their beloved Ms. Leola.

I'd experienced occasions like this before but never with so large a gathering of family members. It was a scene right out of the Waltons. I was thankful to have been a part of such a wonderful time.

For many Americans, Thanksgiving is a special moment in time for family and friends to come together and reflect on the year's blessings.

On that Thanksgiving Day in 2002, I felt generations of "present moments." Sometimes we get so caught up thinking about the things we don't have or places we haven't been that we forget what we do have. There are many overlooked blessings in the simplicity of life: the afternoon sunshine, dinner with your spouse, having lunch with your child at school (particularly while they're young and it's cool to do), talking on the telephone with a favorite aunt or uncle, a tranquil Saturday afternoon without the feeling of needing to have a to-do list in order to make the weekend a success; watching your child smile with joy after she's accomplished a task. These are the things I'm thankful for.

What about you? What are you thankful for? Who are you thankful for? Have you given it some thought? This is a perfect time to reflect on the abundance in your life, and I know you have some. Why don't you take a moment and think about it?

The Simplicity of Youth

The valued servant leadership qualities, characteristics, or virtues have a certain simplicity to them. Servant leadership authors and speakers use words such as humility, relationships, caring, and trust. Servant leadership is not a complicated philosophy. It *is* a lifelong journey and it will take your best efforts to draw forth your servant leadership qualities. Perhaps it will help to examine your past. Think back to the person you were before you became wise to the ways of the world. I like to remember the humility, relationships, caring, and trust that were embodied in Christmas breaks as a child.

In retrospect, life was uncomplicated as a kid. I was too young to work, and I didn't have a care in the world. Two weeks out of school for holiday break seemed like an eternity. Few homes in our neighborhood were decorated like the Griswolds in Chevy Chase's *A Christmas Vacation*. The only decoration in our house was the tree. For my little sister and me, the tree was all that mattered.

My Christmas presents were few and easy to operate. There was no such thing as the Xbox, the PlayStation 2, the Nintendo GameCube or the Internet. Our family didn't have 99 cable television channels, so I was not inundated with toy commercials the way kids are today. I did, however, have the Spiegel Christmas Catalogue. I must have peered through that book a hundred times before the holidays. Any toy or game I picked out kept me focused on what gifts we were going to receive—no television commercials necessary.

Our family gathering was a major event. Sometimes it was held on Christmas Eve, but usually it was held on Christmas Day. It was the most festive occasion of the year. Members of our family, five and six generations, would attend. Every child had another child to play with in his or her age group. The food was delightful and the fellowship was memorable.

I remember numerous Christmases when the weather was unseasonably warm. This was great because my friends and I got the chance to spend a lot of time playing outdoors. Each of us had bicycles and would ride them all over the neighborhood. Our usual destination was to play basketball in someone's backyard and we played from sunup to sundown.

Due to my father being the head basketball coach at Central High School, most of my childhood Christmases centered on the William Henry Shaw Christmas Basketball Tournament. It was always held December 26-30 at the old Municipal Auditorium in Columbus, Georgia. If you were a sports fan, it was the place to be. Because Central made it to the tournament finals 13 straight years, it seemed like all of Phenix City would turn out for the event. Family members as far away as Pittsburgh would come home for the holidays just to attend the tournament. The games were always exciting—even the few we lost. Daddy's teams won the tournament nine times, more than any other school. Besides the games themselves, two things I remember most about the tournament were the chili dogs and the scoreboard buzzer at the auditorium.

The joy of my youth was heightened during the Christmas holidays. Playing basketball with my friends, playing with toys and seeing my relatives at family get-togethers and at the Christmas tournament were special times. They were times filled with the essence of the simplicity of life.

A Call to Serve

In one of bestselling author Dennis Kimbro's books, he begins the chapter on desire by saying, "In everyone's life there comes a time of ultimate challenge—a time when all our resources are tested. A time when life seems unfair. A time when our faith, our values, our patience, our compassion, our ability to persist, are all pushed to the limit and beyond." I would imagine that the residents of New Orleans are feeling this testing in the aftermath of the devastation and destruction left by Hurricane Katrina.

There's no doubt that the people of New Orleans and certain parts of Mississippi and Alabama are being challenged. In many respects, our whole nation is being challenged. On September 11, 2001, we were faced with terrorist attacks.

The terrible tragedy unleashed by Hurricane Katrina has caused understandable bewilderment. People my age have never seen such a natural disaster take place. I never thought I would see this type of tragedy happen in America and so close to home. Nearly everyone in our area was impacted, from the businesses and churches to local governments and school systems.

It was nice to see our young people so eager to lend a helping hand to those in need. A principal at one local school told me that one of her students was watching the aftermath of Katrina on television with his mother. When the mom became emotional and started to cry, her child looked at her and asked, "Mom, are you going to cry or are you going to do something?" That's quite a spirit coming from a child.

With all of this heartfelt support and thoughts from our young people, I get a little perplexed when I hear the responses of some adults. One friend of mine told me he wanted to help out but didn't have any ideas, so he went to a local organization seeking answers. Likeminded people were already there when he arrived; however, for the first 30 minutes all the director talked about was how thankful he was because "it could have been us."

While I am extremely grateful that the people of our community escaped the wrath of Hurricane Katrina, somehow I can't help but wonder if "it could have been us" is a selfish thought. I strongly believe that our thoughts and actions need to be on those in need and not on ourselves.

Many of the greatest leaders in the history of this world were never concerned with their own well-being. The powerful and prophetic words spoken by President John F. Kennedy at his inaugural address in 1961 speak volumes to us today. "Ask not what your country can do for you; ask what you can do for your country." In the wake of 9/11 and Hurricane Katrina, we should all pay heed to these timeless words and do our part to serve those who are in need.

Dare to Dream

A couple of years ago, I had the opportunity to conduct a workshop for the Dare to Dream Summit. I was a little apprehensive about presenting to teenagers because I didn't know how they would respond to the topic or me. But their energy and the events of the day before inspired me to give my best.

The Dare to Dream Summit is an annual event sponsored by Leadership Columbus (Georgia) Alumni. The event is jointly sponsored with the Muscogee County School District and the civic organization One Columbus. High school students are free to engage in dialogue about diversity and race relations. More than 100 students participated in that year's event.

I wondered if I was capable of getting a clear message across to these young people. I didn't know if they were interested in what I had to say but I was curious to hear what was on their minds.

As with most audiences, and particularly with teenagers, there was a "feeling out process." A level of trust had to be established. I thought it was more important for them than for me. Right off the bat I could tell what they were thinking. They wanted to know if I was "being real." That's important to young people today.

That year's Summit centered on the topic of diversity. I was responsible for conducting a "Recognizing Diversity" class. At the beginning of the session, I asked the students to sit next to someone they didn't know. Of course, that's when they began to moan. I explained to them that in life there will come a time when they will have to associate with a person or people they are not comfortable with. I assured the students that this little exercise would be okay and after a while, they agreed. One of the students told me that she enjoyed the experience so much she didn't want to leave the person she'd just met.

From the moment the workshop began, the students' boundless energy and youthful enthusiasm was contagious. Many times an audience will get going based on the energy level of the speaker, but in this case, it was reversed. I fed off of them. I wasn't surprised at how perceptive they were. It was nice to be around young people who had so much to bring to the table.

During the workshop, I asked the students their plans after high school. I could tell by the depth of their answers that many of them had given that question considerable thought. Most of them told me they wanted to make a difference in the world; they were very knowledgeable about current events. They answered every question I posed, and they asked a lot of them, as well.

Though the Summit was successful, it wasn't without sadness. The day before the event a Carver High School student had been shot and killed. There were despondent faces because some of the kids in attendance that morning were from Carver High School. It's devastating to see a young person's life come to an end so early. That's why, as apprehensive as I was before the workshop, I knew that I had to give them my all during the time we spent together.

Part of my life's mission is to show people, whether young or not so young, how to get the most out of their God-given talents so they can make the world a better place. I wanted the teenagers at the Dare to Dream Summit to realize who they are and what they have to offer in this world. My basic message to them on diversity was to embrace their diversity and appreciate as persons those whom they see as "different." I wanted them to understand they all have individual talents and gifts to bring to the table of life.

A Crown of Life

It is not uncommon to attend a servant leadership workshop and be asked to name someone who has made a difference in your life. The second most common question is, "What characteristics did that person display that made such a difference in your life?" For me, the person I always name first is my late grandmother, Essie Mae Brundidge. I have often said that there should be a picture of her in the dictionary under the entry of "grandmother." She was a servant leader before the term was ever coined. The servant leadership characteristics she displayed were numerous.

For the life of me, I cannot ever remember my grandmother greeting me with anything less than a smile. And if I happened to be in another room and had yet to greet her, she would always call me to come give her a hug and a kiss.

Grandmamma Essie Mae was a very giving person. On Sundays after church, people came from miles around to eat dinner at her house, and she loved every minute of it. There was nothing she had that she minded giving away, if you wanted it. One Sunday afternoon, not long before Grandmamma entered hospice, my mother went to visit her. At the time, I was in graduate school. When my mother returned home, she called to tell me that Grandmamma had given her $20 to give me for school. That was the type of person she was— always giving and always caring.

Grandmamma was also an excellent teacher. She taught Sunday school at St. Peter A.M.E. Church in Seale, Alabama for decades. She had that special touch and always knew just what to say. My first couple of years in college were not the best for me. In fact, at that time in my life, I really didn't enjoy school all that much. I didn't like going to class, and my grades plummeted. I basically had no goals. My parents were afraid I was headed in the wrong direction and wouldn't find my way back; however, Grandmamma brought me back to the right path with our long talks. One day she told me about a man named King Solomon and how much he valued wisdom. She told me that he could have had anything he wanted in this world and he asked for wisdom. She told me I should read the Book of Proverbs, and I did. And to this day, whether in good times or bad, I always read this book of the Bible.

When I discussed my problems with Grandmamma, she would say, "Kelvin, be of good courage." Grandmamma always had courage. Even as she was dying of cancer she tried her best to enjoy life. Just days before she entered hospice, she amazed us all as she mustered up enough energy to attend a Sunday night church service. Grandmamma has been gone now for three years. It has pretty much taken me this long to talk about her without tearing up. I'm okay now and even though she is no longer with me physically, I can still feel her presence in everything I do. The lessons she taught my sister, my cousins and me will last for generations. Grandmamma Essie Mae Brundidge's favorite gospel song was, "There's a Crown of Life Waiting for Me." And that's exactly what she was, "A Crown of Life."

Centers for Servant Leadership

About the Greenleaf Center for Servant Leadership

The Greenleaf Center for Servant Leadership was founded in 1964 by Robert K. Greenleaf, who launched the modern servant leadership movement in 1970 with the publication of his classic essay, "The Servant as Leader." The Greenleaf Center is an international non-profit organization dedicated to promoting the awareness, understanding, and practice of servant leadership by individuals and organizations. The vision of the Center is: "Across our global community, servant leadership is embraced as a guiding principle, thus building a more just, caring, and sustainable world with hope and prosperity for future generations."

The Greenleaf Center hosts an annual international conference, retreats, and the Leadership Institute for Education (LIFE) conference. Services of the Center include a speakers bureau, Greenleaf Seminars, the Greenleaf Scholars Program, and the Greenleaf Academy. The Center also publishes books and essays, and sells servant leadership resources through its online catalog.

To become a member or donor, or to learn more about the Center's services, please contact the Center at:

The Greenleaf Center for Servant Leadership
770 Pawtucket Drive
Westfield, IN 46074
Tel. 317-669-8050
Fax 317-669-8055
www.greenleaf.org

About The Center for Servant Leadership at the Pastoral Institute

The Center for Servant Leadership at the Pastoral Institute in Columbus, Georgia is committed to creating and sustaining servant leadership throughout organizations and institutions. The Center for Servant Leadership endeavors to advance the development of a caring and cooperating community, emphasizing services and involvement, a balanced approach to life and work, and a sharing of responsibility and recognition. Its programs and partnerships help develop attitudes and skills of servant leaders among civic and community organizers, business managers and professionals, college students, teenagers, and children.

William B. Turner, author of *The Learning of Love: A Journey Toward Servant Leadership*, has truly been the father of the servant leadership movement in the Columbus, Georgia area. The Pastoral Institute was founded in 1974 as a community-based organization by a group of servant leaders with Turner serving as Chairman of the Board. The Pastoral Institute offers faith-based counseling, education and consultation services to the community. In 2003 the Pastoral Institute affiliated with the Samaritan Institute based in Denver, Colorado and in 1994 and 2004 the Pastoral Institute was selected by the American Association of Pastoral Counselors as the premier program in the nation.

The Pastoral Institute reaches out to the region through its services to organizations, congregations, and businesses by offering a wide variety of programs designed to strengthen individuals and families.

Committed to the holistic perspective that values mind, body, spirit and community, the Pastoral Institute continues to provide help, hope and healing to those seeking our services.

For more information, please contact:
The Center for Servant Leadership
Pastoral Institute
2022 Fifteenth Avenue, Columbus, GA 31901
Tel. 706-649-6500, Fax 706-649-6521
www.pastoralinstitute.org

Acknowledgments

I want to thank my wife, Faye, and our daughters, Kristina and Kirsten. I love you dearly, and everything that I do, I do for you. Mom and Dad, thank you for loving me and showing me the way. To my Aunt Geri for being my cheerleader. To my Uncle Larry for keeping me grounded in reality. I want to thank my colleagues at the Pastoral Institute for their support and encouragement. To Fran for always encouraging me to write the book. To Ron for your guidance and support. To Stephen for your inspiration and shoulder to cry on. My thanks to Kent Keith and the Greenleaf Center for Servant Leadership for making this dream a reality. To Beth, my favorite editor, and to Kimberly and Kelli for picking up the slack. To Heidi Newman for what I hope is the beginning of a beautiful friendship. To the late Lynn Drury, a mentor whose lessons will never be forgotten. Last but surely not least to Jean who has been with me on the journey every step of the way—you are absolutely wonderful.

About the Author

Kelvin Redd is the Director of the Center for Servant Leadership at the Pastoral Institute in Columbus, Georgia. He is a featured leadership facilitator, keynote speaker, Emergenetics Associate, and professional business coach. Kelvin writes a monthly newsletter, *Servant Leadership Today.* He has hosted a television show on servant leadership and has been a college adjunct instructor.

Kelvin received a Bachelor of Arts in history from Auburn University and holds a Master of Science in Management degree, with a concentration in Leadership and Organizational Effectiveness, from Troy University. He has completed postgraduate studies at the University of Georgia's Terry College of Business. For 13 years, Kelvin worked for Synovus Financial Corporation in Columbus, Georgia, a company rated by *Fortune* magazine as "The Best Place to Work in America" in 1999. He was promoted to an assistant vice president in 1995.

Kelvin has presented workshops and speeches to thousands of people in businesses, colleges, universities, and civic organizations throughout the country, including Aflac, the Synovus Leadership Institute, and the Greenleaf Center International Conference. He delivered the 2008 Chattahoochee Valley Community College Commencement address.

Kelvin has served in numerous leadership capacities throughout his professional career, such as Leadership Columbus Class of 2005-06, president of the Columbus-Phenix City Auburn Club, Phenix City Rotary Club, the Servant Leadership Advisory Council of Brookstone School, Phenix City Planning Commission, Auburn University Board of Trustees Alumni Advisory Council, Muscogee County Chapter of the American Red Cross, Kiwanis Club of North Columbus, and the Phenix-Russell Boys and Girls Club.